MW01101353

BE A
MASTER™
OF
SELF LOVE

DR. KOUSOULI'S *33* MASTER SECRETS TO LOVING YOUR EXTRAORDINARY LIFE

Dr. Theodoros Kousouli

A Personal Empowerment Book

Kousouli Enterprises
Los Angeles, CA

Copyright © 2016 by Theodoros Kousouli D.C., CHt.

All rights reserved. No part of this book may be reproduced or utilized in any form or by any means, electronic or mechanical including photocopying, recording, or by any information storage and retrieval system, without permission in writing from the author and publisher, except for the inclusion of brief quotations in a review with proper credit cited.

The BE A MASTER™ BOOK SERIES (http://www.BEAMASTER.com) trademarked brand and work is Copyright of Dr. Theodoros Kousouli.

The KOUSOULI® mark and the Kousouli® Method 4R Intervention health system are registered trademarks of Theodoros D. Kousouli D.C., CHt. and Kousouli Enterprises.

Heartfelt gratitude to the following for their contributions:
Editing & research assistance: Latasha Doyle
Layout coordinator: Gustavo Martinez
Cover images of Dr. Kousouli and internal photography: Matthew A. Cooke
Cover heart image: Shutter Stock; Nils Z

ISBN: 978-0997627657   Softcover
ISBN: 978-0997627664   Epub
ISBN: 978-0997627671   Kindle

Library of Congress Control Number: 2016909172

Kousouli Enterprises
P.O. Box 360494
Los Angeles, CA 90036

Printed in the United States of America

CONTENTS

Life Changing Products · Books · Seminars · Empowerment CD's · Get on the Newsletter!
Connect with Dr. Kousouli, www.DrKousouli.com and on all Social Media Platforms
@DrKousouli #DrKousouli #KousouliMethod
You Will Also Enjoy Dr. Kousouli's Other Published Works
Available Now from Major Retailers:

BE A MASTER™ OF MAXIMUM HEALING
How to Lead a Healthy Life Without Limits
- Holistic Solutions for Over <u>60</u> Diseases to Help You and Your Loved Ones Heal!

BE A MASTER™ OF PSYCHIC ENERGY
Your Key to Truly Mastering Your Personal Power
- Uncover and Amplify Your Hidden Psychic Abilities to Change Your Life!

BE A MASTER™ OF SEX ENERGY
Hypnotize Your Partner for Love and Great Sex
- Build a Stronger Bond with Your Lover(s) Using Subconscious Science!

BE A MASTER™ OF SUCCESS
Dr. Kousouli's 33 Master Secrets to Achieving Your Dreams
- Solid Success Principles You can Apply Right Now to Empower Your Life!

BE A MASTER™ OF SELF IMAGE
Dr. Kousouli's 33 Master Secrets to Living Healthier, Happier and Hotter
- Simple Holistic Tips & Tricks for More Weight Loss and Body Benefit to You!

If you would like to share your story of how Dr. Kousouli's books, CDs or seminars have impacted your life for the better, we would love to hear from you! (Messages are screened by staff and forwarded when appropriate.)

For A Free Gift from Dr. Theo Kousouli visit www.FreeGiftFromDrTheo.com

DISCLAIMER

In a land where being politically correct seems more 'right' than standing for the 'truth,' or more desired than expressing an honest opinion, it's sad that I must digress and add the following legal disclaimer to remind you, the reader, that *you must think for yourself.*

This book is a collection of experiences and research that form my thoughts, opinions, and conclusions as a board certified Doctor of Chiropractic (D.C.) and Hypnotherapist (CHt); not a Doctor of Medicine (M.D.). The content herein is controversial as it presents an alternate view to the status quo. There are establishments who may disagree with certain contents of this book, and would have preferred that this information never found your eyes. However, this book is not intended for them; it was written for the countless individuals yearning for better health and well-being amongst a society that has lost its way.

The writings in this book are based on my personal research, experience, interpretations, and beliefs. Your personal beliefs will affect your ability to review this material, as you will put it through your own filters. I intend to guide you in developing your own ability to use your personal energy in a healthy manner, and this book is a guide for you to grow, but is not by any means the final word on the subject.

I encourage you, the reader, to research, analyze, and develop your own opinions on the subject matters discussed. As a holistic health care provider, I express the truth as I have come to know it. It is my duty to aid in the growth of my beloved patients, family, and friends with this love so they too may reach the heights of what their Creator made possible for them to be.

Theodoros Kousouli D.C., CHt.

LEGAL DISCLAIMER

This publication is for informational purposes only. The material presented herein denotes the views of the author as of the date of press. The material and ideas provided herein are believed to be truthful and complete, based on the author's best judgment and experience, formed from the available data at the time of publication. Because of the speed by which conditions and information change, the author reserves the right to amend and update his opinions at any time based upon the new data and circumstances. While every effort has been made to provide complete, accurate, current, and reliable information within this publication, no warranties of any kind are expressed or implied. The publisher, author, and all associated parties involved with this publication assume no responsibility for errors, inaccuracies, oversights, or conflicting interpretations of the content herein. The author and publisher do not accept any responsibility for any liabilities resulting from the use of this information. Readers acknowledge that the author is not engaging in rendering guarantees of income or outcome of any kind in connection with using any methods, techniques, or information stated or implied. Any perceived results of the material's use can vary greatly per case and individual circumstance. Mention of any persons or companies in this book does not imply that they endorse this book, its content, or the author, and similarly the author does not endorse them. Any supposed slights of specific establishments, corporations, organizations, peoples, or persons are unintended.

You should consult your own chiropractor, acupuncturist, herbalist, naturopath, hypnotherapist or other holistic doctor(s) in combination with sound medical advice. Readers are cautioned to first consult with proper health professionals about their individual circumstances on any matter relating to their health and personal well-being, prior to taking any course of action. The author is not a licensed medical doctor or psychiatrist and the *information provided in this book should not be construed as personal, medical, or psychiatric advice or instruction.* All readers or users of the information herein, who fail to consult proper health experts, assume the risk of any and all injuries. **The contents of this book and the information herein have not been evaluated or approved by the Food and Drug Administration for the treatment or cure of any disease, disorder, syndrome, or ailment mentioned herein.**

This book is dedicated to my mother who gave limitless love to my siblings and I, and to all the mothers who have loved and nurtured their children so they may be sustained in their journeys.

"A praying mother is more precious and valuable than all the riches in the world."
~ Violet James

Introduction

"That is all I want in life: for this pain to seem purposeful."
~ *Elizabeth Wurtzel*

As I finish writing this book, I find myself about to undergo my second major heart operation. It's been ten years since my first one, and my, how the time has flown. It's ironic to be writing a book about loving yourself as I find my currently installed prosthetic aortic bovine valve deteriorating ...and I find myself back in the same place I was in just ten years ago, having to receive a new valve to extend my life on this planet. I have many mixed feelings just as before, but this time I am without distress. Instead, I feel grateful for the last ten years, as my life has been lived so thoroughly compared to the twenty-eight years before my first surgery. The last decade has been extremely humbling, and enlightening in regards to learning how everything works in life, this world, and the universe. I have come to the conclusion there is only one truth: Love. All else is an illusionary lie.

I wrote this book for the people, like myself, who have struggled with self-love, depression, and who have looked high and low for a source of positivity in a seemingly negative world. Over my journey, and even before my first heart surgery, I had started searching for ways to overcome obstacles that many of us share. Like many people growing up, I didn't feel a lot of emotional stability within my family, even though we were considered entirely "normal" by society's standards. I grew up in a traditional family: my super religious mother, my military-minded father, and my twin siblings. The three of us were raised with "tough love," and my Greek mother stayed home to take care of us. However, that love did not come without "invisible" strings attached. Those invisible strings, although unintentional, challenged my emotional stability all the way into adulthood.

My father wasn't around much because he worked so hard; he owned a restaurant and as a strict, tough, proud Greek ex-merchant marine, he felt his job was to provide for us financially, which was enough "work" to be considered a good father. All stress from a rough day at work, was by default taken out on my siblings, my mother, and me. A hard working man indeed, he had little understanding how balance in life was needed when raising a family. After all, he and his own parents lived through WWII in Greece, where life was extremely tough, and where "perfect" parenting took a backseat to surviving Nazi rule. And so I grew up without him in a sense; no tossing the football in the backyard after work, no showing me how to stand up for myself, nor was he there for me when I was bullied for years at school. Now I see how important it is for a boy growing up to have both parental figures fully present in his life. It took me a long time to understand that physical presence isn't the same as emotional access.

Other struggles in my life became evident as I grew to be a teenager and young adult, when I found it hard to experience love in my other relationships. I didn't realize at the time that the constant fighting, name-calling, yelling, and rage my parents exhibited in front of their children would severely impact my thoughts on dating, love and marriage. I was also bullied by larger classmates for much of my childhood and adolescence, to the point of physical attacks. Back then, nobody did much about bullying, so I was forced to crawl deep within myself and try to survive.

Around the time I reached middle school, I also began having dreams and visions that I couldn't exactly decipher; they made me feel crazy and entirely "other." I quickly learned to not discuss these with anyone, as I was already subject to enough emotional abuse. One day after a particularly terrible day at school, I arrived home, drained and ready to end it all. I picked up a razor, intent on ridding myself of this pain; I couldn't take it anymore. As I pressed the razor blade to my wrist though, I heard a strong inner voice shout "NO!"

This stern yet loving voice, while I didn't know where it came from at the time, saved my life. It gave me the clarity to see that my environment was toxic and that the bullies and people around me were the ones affecting me. I was not crazy, and I could get through this. Of course, it wasn't that easy, but it was a starting point.

Between the religious dogmatic control from my mother, who is Orthodox in all that she does and teaches, and the lack of emotional support from a positive, encouraging father figure, I was left with very little to go on when I left the nest. I knew what my parents had (or had not) taught me, but that wasn't enough to get by in the world "out there."

Essentially, I had to ask the right questions to find my own light and answers to life. You, the reader, are probably dealing with similar struggles if you've picked up this book. You probably don't have the emotional support that you need, whether it's a parent or another important figure in your life, so you're seeking answers on your own. Whatever your reason is for not fully loving yourself, whether it's a tough upbringing, a series of incredibly unfortunate circumstances, abusive relationships, body image struggles, or virtually any other reason, that's your old story.

But the purpose of this book is to help you understand your old story, let it go, and write many new exciting chapters. We are all born with certain circumstances that affect our lives, and we're moved into even more as we grow up. When you were not raised with, or do not have access to, the support you need to thrive, it makes it difficult to function in a very demanding society, where you have so many things coming at you.

My hope is that with this book, you will take a time-out, put your old story aside, take a deep breath, and read this material with an optimistic, open mind. To great effect, the tips that follow in this book are what I used to pull myself out of difficult times. I know they will help you, too.

Lessons I've Learned

Despite the constant dogmatic church talk and "going to Hell if you misbehave" lectures from my mother, one thing that really stuck with me was the parable of the talents in Matthew 25:14-30. In this parable, a Lord (who represents God) is about to go away on a journey and He entrusts his talents (represented in the parable as money and coins) to three of his servants (representing us humans) according to their ability. When he returned from the trip, he asked his three servants to present the talents he had bestowed upon them for safekeeping.

One servant, who was given five talents, returned with five talents more! The one who was given two talents returned with two more. To them their Lord said, "Well *done,* good and faithful servant." They were faithful and loyal with these talents, so he granted them rule over more blessings in his kingdom. However, the last servant who was given one talent hid it out of fear and laziness, and returned only the one talent back to his Lord. The favor of God was with the two other servants, who yielded back profit from what the Lord had given to them, and the last was cast away.

The lesson of the parable was clear to me; find what you have been gifted with and reproduce that in the Glory of your Maker. Joy and abundance in life are given to those who clearly see and make the most of their life, for even if it is little, you will be given more. And those who squander their God-given abilities will weep and feel despair in life.

Whether you believe in the benevolent energies of creation or not, I have come to the understanding that despite "Man" (and all Man has gotten wrong), God does love you. I am not talking about

Church or the idea of a religious God. I am not talking about a Bible-thumping, rolling-on-the-floor, dancing like a chicken, television preaching, mankind version of God. No. I am talking about that which transcends all of Man's notions of the Almighty; the energy that beats in your heart right now, the energy that gives you the breath you're taking, and the ability to turn words on a page into living information you can use to change your life forever. I'm talking about *that* God. That's the God that loves you, and wants nothing but love and joy for you. But we must uncover what Man has placed between where you are and where you want to be. That's where we begin with this book.

IN THIS BOOK, YOU WILL LEARN:

- ✓ How to rewrite your story; be the author, not the character!
- ✓ How to break through depression and regain control of your life
- ✓ How to build super self-esteem that will let you cultivate self-love
- ✓ How to live an extraordinary life, no matter your "old" story
- ✓ Tips and tactics to uplift your mood when you're down
- ✓ Holistic alternatives and supplements to replace drugs and remove dependency (work closely with your doctors)
- ✓ How diet and food can affect your mood and spirit
- ✓ Ways to create positive energy around you
- ✓ Ways to avoid negative input
- ✓ How much your body, mind, and spirit are connected
- ✓ Ways to explore your past and forgive yourself and others in order to move forward to a brighter future
- ✓ And so much more!

Chapter One:
Defining and Addressing Depression

"Your task is not to seek for Love, but merely to seek and find all the barriers within yourself that you have built against it."
~ Rumi

Depression is a mental and emotional state of feeling disconnected from life, and is often accompanied with overpowering feelings of sadness, apathy, gloom, and hopelessness. Some say it is caused by chemical and energetic changes in the brain and spinal cord, while other times it starts following a traumatic event or change in life. It's important to note that periods of sadness and anxiety are normal for *everybody*. However, it becomes pathologic (a condition that changes the mental and physical environment) when it interferes with important aspects of life, such as school or work, relationships, or the ability to function on a daily basis.

Depression affects over 350 million people worldwide according to the World Health Organization– and those are just the diagnosed cases. The Depression and Bipolar Support Alliance says depression is more prevalent among females, affecting up to 25% of women and 12% of men in the United States. There are also connections to other illnesses, like anxiety or bipolar disorders, and can often be a by-product of illegal (as well as legal) drug use.

What Does the Medical Community do for Depression?

While I'm not trying to bash the medical community, or disregard the benefits that some people get from medications and psychiatry, I do know that it's certainly not the only path. I myself have been on this journey, and was frustrated by the labels, the treatments, and the assumptions that the medical world's treatment would "cure me." Their ways, in my humble opinion, are frequently far more expensive, risky and less effective than other natural, safer options. It's important to understand exactly what the medical community provides to treat depression, however, so you can make an educated decision about what is right for you.

Many people also seek psychological or psychiatric advice. What's the difference? A psychologist with a Ph.D. , Psy.D., or Ed.D, is most likely going to explore how you've gotten to this point, give you specific tools or activities that can help you work through your depression, and so on. A psychiatrist is a doctor with either a M.D. or D.O. degree, with training in the field of psychiatry which can (and usually does) prescribe medications that severely affect blood chemistry and personality.

Popular Medications for Depression

- **Selective serotonin reuptake inhibitors (SSRIs).** According to mayoclinic.org, SSRI medications like paroxetine (Paxil, Pexeva), fluoxetine (Prozac), citalopram (Celexa), escitalopram (Lexapro), and sertraline (Zoloft) are the drugs most doctors try first when treating depression. *Some* side effects include: nausea, reduced libido, insomnia, lethargy, weight gain, headaches, and suicidal thoughts.

- **Serotonin-norepinephrine reuptake inhibitors (SNRIs).** SNRIs include venlafaxine (Effexor XR), duloxetine (Cymbalta), levomilnacipran (Fetzima), and desvenlafaxine (Khedezla, Pristiq). *Some* side effects include nausea, dizziness, sweating, anxiety, constipation, and decreased sex drive.

- **Norepinephrine-dopamine reuptake inhibitors (NDRIs).** Bupropion medications (Wellbutrin, Forfivo XL, Aplenzin) are one of the few antidepressants without sexual side effects, and Wellbutrin is also used to cut smoking cravings. Weight gain and sedation/lethargy are common.

- **New medications.** Mirtazapine (Remeron), and Trazodone are used as a sedative, usually in combination with an antidepressant that gives you insomnia. Newer medications include vortioxetine (Brintellix) and vilazodone (Viibryd) are recommended because they don't kill sex drive.

- **Tricyclic antidepressants.** Medications like imipramine (Tofranil), nortriptyline (Pamelor), doxepin, amitriptyline, desipramine (Norpramin), trimipramine (Surmontil), and protriptyline (Vivactil) give severe side effects compared to newer drug options. Weight gain, lowered blood pressure, sweating, blurred vision, suicidal ideation, and more can result from taking them.

- **Monoamine oxidase inhibitors (MAOIs).** MAOIs - like phenelzine (Nardil), tranylcypromine (Parnate), and isocarboxazid (Marplan) are usually given when other medicines haven't given results. Often seen as a last resort because they can have serious side effects. Using MAOIs necessitates a stringent diet due to *deadly* (!) interactions with foods (mostly fermented ones like cheese, wine, etc.). Cannot be taken with medications like decongestants, birth control pills, etc. Also causes insomnia, stomach upset, dry mouth, and more.

Because most antidepressants do not work perfectly on their own, doctors usually recommend adding mood stabilizers (antipsychotics) or mingling two antidepressants together. Anti-anxiety and stimulant medications also may be added for short-term use to prevent you from being too "foggy." Basically, more and more medications will be piled on top until they find the right "cocktail" for your system(s).

I don't know about you, but taking a medication that 1.) could make my symptoms worse, and 2.) give me symptoms I've never had - doesn't sound like that effective of a method. Worse yet, long-term studies of people who use antidepressants for long periods of time have found that as many as 23% of people have developed irritable bowel syndrome, or similar digestive conditions. Higher risk of seizure, heart abnormalities, and immunity issues (the drug no longer works for you) have all been reported, according to a *U.S. News* article written by Michael O. Schroeder in 2015.

Stomach problems are the least of your worries, however, because negative violent thoughts, suicidal ideation, and more are very common when patients are on cocktails of antidepressant psychotropic drugs. According to an April 2013 article by Dan Roberts of Ammoland.com, "Nearly every mass shooting incident in the last twenty years, and multiple other instances of suicide and isolated shootings all share one thing in common, and it's not the weapons used.... All of the perpetrators were either actively taking powerful psychotropic drugs or had been at some point in the immediate past before they committed their crimes."

The side effects of all the aforementioned drugs must be taken seriously. They are no joke! Psychotropic drugs, many believe, actually open dimensional portals of altered reality and work in changing perceptual reality. Talk to your doctors and discuss the legitimate risks of any medication you (or they) might want to try. No one has the exact same chemical makeup, so using one drug for everyone's diagnosed "disease" is not treating the individual properly. If the pain issue is not dealt with at the same vibrational level at which it was created, the drug will only cause more problems or symptoms than when you started.

If you have any doubts, get second and third opinions from naturopathic and holistic doctors who can help you properly detox your body of chemicals and drugs. You can also try the non-drug activities in this book, as their long-term side effects only include happiness, increased self-love, and an ability to function in life better than ever before.

I also discuss a few holistic health approaches in this book, starting with what I believe is the most important thing you can do for your body and nervous system, in order to remove stress and regulate everything from mental impulses to major body organs.

Dr. Kousouli's Secret Loving Self Tip #1
GET CHIROPRACTIC ADJUSTMENTS REGULARLY

The very first structures that form after conception are the brain and spinal cord. This is the nervous system, which sends instruction to develop the rest of you! As a chiropractor, I'm constantly astounded when people don't realize the connection between their brain, spinal cord, and body. Most of the time, when there is a problem somewhere in your body, there usually is a spinal or nerve interference issue that needs to be addressed. Much tension is held in the upper part of the spine and can cause many upper head problems, like cervicogenic headaches which will bring on things like brain fog, pain, double vision, fatigue, and decreased productivity. Then the person experiencing these symptoms will ask their medical doctor for medications or even a referral to a psychiatrist because they may be also having a hard time with work, family, marriage, etc. Eventually the slippery slope leads to prescribed drug use and dependency due to mental malpractice and the mantra, "a pill for every ill," among medical doctors. Many of these situations can be easily helped (and many bad circumstances prevented) with the application of lifestyle and diet changes, as well as chiropractic therapy to destress the nervous system.

Although these words may not make sense to you, talk to your Chiropractor about analyzing and adjusting the Occiput, C1 - C4; T5- T10 and L1-S1 spinal levels, which cover the majority of stress removal from organ points in the body. Most chiropractors should be able to also recommend a good aerobic exercise, supplementation, and diet program. The amount of stress that leaves from correct application of chiropractic therapy is unbelievable. It is like defragmenting a computer hard drive so that the system can function better and perform faster. This may be the breath of fresh air your mental and physical health has been yearning for.

When your brain is able to send messages properly from your body to your brain and back again without interference, you can begin to work on the emotional and spiritual aspects of your mental health. Without addressing the spinal connection first, you're essentially depriving yourself of a major tool you can use in rebalancing very important chemicals and neurotransmitters in your body. Think about it; if your brain isn't firing properly, how are all the feel-good transmitters like dopamine, oxytocin, and norepinephrine supposed to get to work? This is especially necessary if you've been on neuro-toxic medications for depression or other issues in the past, which leads into the next point:

Dr. Kousouli's Secret Loving Self Tip #2
DETOXIFYING AND REMOVING TOXIC CHEMICALS

Think back to when a healthy baby is born; does the baby come out of the womb holding prescription pills? Do we give a sick, wilting plant Prozac - or do we know it needs natural sun and water? So why do doctors think we "need" so many drugs to find our natural happiness or lead a healthy life? Could it be marketing madness thanks to Big Pharma over decades of hard-core advertising? Indeed it is.

Ask your doctors about cutting back prescribed drug dosages and checking possible other drug interactions. It's very important to do your own research here, as many doctors and pharmacists are only human (they do and will make mistakes), and are notorious for hardly ever checking a patient's prescription or over-the-counter interactions. It never ceases to amaze me when new patient referrals come into my office, who use drugs their medical doctors prescribed for them, and who do not even know the side effects! The patient blindly takes pill after pill, and has no clue that the long list of detrimental side effects is what is actually causing their agony.

For example, depression is a very common side effect of oral contraception, and poor heart medication dosages can lead to increased anxiety or feelings of impending doom. Who knows - maybe you'll find that one of your medications is directly impacting your ability to be happy and healthy. Actually, this may be the Number One problem of an otherwise healthy, happy person. Check your medicines!

Consider holistic avenues, like an herbal cleanse, plant-based diets, and look into kidney, liver, candida, parasite, and heavy metal cleansing through chelation therapy. Refer to my book, BE A MASTER™ OF MAXIMUM HEALING for more information. Another thing I want to make very clear is that your body may actually have a food and vitamin deficiency of some sort, whether from a natural inclination or from a medical interaction. The only way you'll know is if you remove the things from your body that can make you worse. Then, you can get tested for nutritional deficiencies by a naturopath and add supplements to help you improve even more. Let's explore some natural options.

Dr. Kousouli's Secret Loving Self Tip #3
USE NATURAL SUPPLEMENTS TO HELP DEPRESSION

Disclaimer: **Please note that side effects may exist with natural herbs. Proper care is needed for correct administration and use.** Everyone's situation is different. Do not mix supplements or herbs with medications you are already taking, without first checking with your primary health care provider(s) for your specific needs. Some herbs should not be taken by those with certain diseases, or by women who are pregnant or nursing. The following information is provided to you for educational purposes only, and as a general synopsis of possible options that should be discussed with your doctor(s). All readers should consult their own appropriate health professionals for more information, instruction, dosage, and any other matter relating to their personal health and well-being. The information has not been evaluated or approved by the Food and Drug Administration for the treatment or cure of any disease, disorder, syndrome, or ailment mentioned herein. Reader uses this and all information herein at their own risk.

- *St. John's Wort:* Believed to help with depression and is helpful in relieving exhaustion and tension. Must not be mixed with other drugs. There are liquid, capsules, and even tea, but be very careful with the dosages after consulting with your doctor(s).

- *Noni (Morinda)* and *Schisandra:* Powerful natural antidepressants that work on the adrenal glands to prevent fatigue. Also believed to help anxiety and insomnia.

- *Ginkgo Biloba:* Recommended for brain stimulation, memory, and basic brain function. May help treat depression and anxiety by helping chemicals balance.

- *Inositol:* Vitamin B-8, a substance found in many foods (legumes), can help reduce anxiety, depression, and tension.

- *Vitamin B Complex: B3, B5, B6, B12, Vitamin C, Magnesium,* and *Folic Acid:* Making sure you're not deficient in any of these vitamins and minerals is incredibly important.

If you are, eat food that will get you your daily balance, or find a natural supplement. Reaching healthy levels in these can help your brain function better, and your body can process toxins that can lead to nutritional imbalances.

- *Laetrile; Vitamin B 17:* Believed by many holistic experts to be a strong anticancer vitamin that supports a healthy immune system and provides the basis for health; sources are: peach and apricot seeds, clover, millet, buckwheat, barley, flax, blueberries, blackberries, strawberries, bean sprouts, lima beans, sorghum and macadamia nuts to name a few.

- *Kava - Kava:* A good muscle relaxer. Has been shown to help with general stress, depression, and insomnia. Good for short term use only.

- *Lemon Balm:* May eliminate digestive disorders associated with depression. Smell also calms anxiety, and helps with headaches and palpitations caused by it as well.

- *Rhodiola Rosea:* May improve mood, readjusts serotonin and dopamine levels, and increases mental clarity to help remove "depression fog."

- *Vitamin D3:* Depression patients tend to be deficient, which can result in lethargy, weight gain, high blood pressure, insomnia, etc. Sit outside for a few minutes each day! Huge deficiencies can be alleviated with sun exposure and a D3 supplement. More on this later in the book.

- *Omega 3 Fatty Acids EPA/DHA:* Increases anti-inflammatory prostaglandins. Cod liver oil studies have been directly connected to a decrease in depression, suicidality, and stress in various research experiments. Very important for proper brain function.

- **S-adenosylmethionine (SAMe):** Mood enhancer and anti-depressant. Boosts levels of serotonin, dopamine, and nor-epinephrine. Also contributes to antioxidant production, which eliminates free radicals that can cause toxicity and dis-ease.

- **Hydroxytryptophan (5HTP):** Increases serotonin levels and may decrease pain symptoms. Also prevents fatigue by balancing melatonin in the depressed individual.

- **Siberian Ginseng:** Helps the body fight stress reactions by balancing the adrenal glands. Increases mental performance and mood stability.

While these are generalized summaries of the supplements available to you, I recommend that you do your own research, talk to holistic health professionals that you trust, and find a system that is best for you. Much of what is listed above is available in the food you eat, which is why I strongly recommend a well rounded plant-based diet and getting all vitamins from foods first before looking to supplements.

The important thing to know here is that sometimes, no matter how much we want it to help, traditional methods and medications we've tried just aren't doing the trick. There are other alternatives out there not given to you by your doctor(s); keep looking and don't settle for synthetic options when there are better, more natural ones for you. I hope the next chapters help you understand that, and give you more tools to help you on your path to truly loving YOU!

Chapter Two:
Overcoming Abuse and Bullying

"When the victim starts feeling more sorry for their bully than themselves; real healing can begin."
~ Dr. Theo Kousouli

Many people reading this book are experiencing extreme feelings of depression, self-loathing, and even suicidal ideations. For some of us, the cause of this is unclear; possibly a familial predisposition, overburdened toxic lifestyle, an unknown imbalance in the body, or a combination of all of the above. For others, it's a result of early abuse, trauma, or childhood struggles that made us feel "less than." Less than smart, less than perfect, less than human, less than worthy… We all have experiences with this sort of thing, but some of us have been raised in and kept in this cycle until we "know" nothing else and this cycle becomes our normal. If you're a victim of abuse or bullying, I want you to know that you're definitely not alone. I also want you to know that abusive and bullying behaviors, whether you experienced it in your family, in your school, at work, or somewhere else in your immediate surroundings, does not have to define you.

Bullying is Never "Normal"

Plenty of people are bullied in school, and some of those people "turn out just fine." In 1998, as an early pioneer of the anti-bully movement, I made a guest speaker appearance on the then-syndicated popular talk show, "Jenny Jones." I confronted one of the bullies from my high school years on national television and received a long overdue apology afterwards in the green room backstage. My message was simple then, and it holds true to this day: someone who is bullied will have his or her life changed forever. Not many people will take the high road to learn and grow from the challenge when confronted with such abuse. When faced with public humiliation, the bully's brushed off defensive response was "We were kids, that's what we did as kids."

But there is a fine line between occasionally being picked on in the lunchroom and being physically or emotionally bullied into terror and submission every day. I want readers to know that bullying is a mind virus that is taught and passed through family and social structures in our society and in every generation since the Caveman and Colosseum Days. It's an old energy, one that promotes the idea, "Only the strong survive." It tries to make us believe that, in order to be loved and respected, you have to be feared. Is this the way of the higher mind, of reason and heartfelt compassion for your fellow man? Of course not. Compare many Caesars and the one Christ: Caesars ruled with malicious tyranny conquering lands, and Christ shared the message of forgiveness and love, bringing the world together. Which ones teachings and message still stand today?

The Good News

The world is transitioning now to a higher, more compassionate vibration; moving away from war and towards building global communities and friendships where our differences are resolved by accepting others. In the United States, much more emphasis has been placed on educating youth on how to identify abuse and bullying through nonprofits, school presentations, and easy access to counseling and resources. When many of us were in school, we recognized the signs of abuse or bullying but were told that, "It doesn't concern us," or, "Don't snitch," so we'd keep our mouths shut.

Schools are now realizing just how bullying starts, and have begun to intervene in the bullies' lives, moreso than their victims. Why? It's not enough to tell Bully Joe not to tease little Tommy. Bully

Joe won't curb his actions at school if he witnesses his father hitting his mother at home; he won't know that his behaviors are unacceptable and come with personal consequences. Bully Joe will likely also hit his sister and anyone smaller than him, not because Bully Joe is inherently a bad kid or person, but because he is learning how to behave in a world he's new in, and he's seeing the actions of adults around him as normal/proper.

Odds are, Bully Joe's grandparents were also "victims" to their own abusive behaviors, and who knows how far back it goes from there. These mind viruses of bullying and abuse start to spread, and they're hard to stop. It's an ongoing loop, and if not deal with swiftly and diligently now, the next generation faces the same fate. The bully will teach his children to bully and abuse, and the victim will learn that they will always be a victim.

Why We Need to Stop Bullying *Now*

Solving the bully problem in the home can save our society on a global scale. America seems to have the biggest bully problem, not only in its schools but also in law, politics and the world stage. The victim and his or her parents (if they are not involved in the abuse/bullying) must act swiftly to neutralize the bullying. The longer it is going on, the harder the resolve later. Involve not just the school, but also the bully and his family in therapy or counseling. Build the victim's support group and let both the bully and the victim know there is zero tolerance for such behavior.

I have also had great success in helping both the bully and the victims using the Kousouli® Method (more on this in Chapter 6), which wonderfully rehabilitates the bully's early trauma, and brings back homeostasis to the victim's loss of personal power. Please keep in mind that bullying isn't just a playground phenomenon. We're bullied in our homes, in our schools, in our workplaces, in our romantic relationships. Bullying and abuse go hand-in-hand (when one does not know and use effectively their personal power), and seeing that connection can save lives.

Other resources:

- If you or someone you know is being abused, please call 911 immediately, or reach out to the Domestic Abuse Hotline at 1-800-799-7233.

- For resources on bullying, including who to contact and what to do, please check out http://www.stopbullying.gov/get-help-now/

- If you are a victim of abuse or bullying and feel that you are a risk to yourself or others, please call 911 immediately or call the National Suicide Prevention Hotline at 1-800-273-TALK.

You can overcome this, and you will learn to forgive (sometimes a very difficult, but very healing act) yourself and those who have wronged you. That is what this book is all about, so let's get started.

Chapter Three:
To Know Thyself Is to Love Yourself

"I am not what has happened to me. I am what I choose to become."
~ Carl Jung

As a person with a story (everyone has a story), you have internalized everything that has happened to you, with you, or even around you. That's what we as children are meant to do; soak up all of our external influences and grow accordingly to the perspective we feel is our "truth". Others involved in the same events will perceive their truth in radically different ways than another in the same event, like witnesses at a car accident scene who all have different stories. But sometimes, we are not given the opportunity to grow in ways that benefit us. Sometimes, our growth is stinted by trauma, by our parents, or even by our geography, race, or resources. Other times, we grow in the "right" direction, only to have our much-needed support system cut out from underneath us, or to experience an event that shakes us to our core.

As we will discuss in depth in Chapter 10, your *story* is the sum total of what has happened to you. **But *you* are not what has happened to you.** In order to fully love yourself, it means to address your story, your past, all of those people and things that make you feel less than worthy of love, and say: "I love myself. That's my new truth. That's my first truth." As with most things worth our time, this is easier said than believed.

Dr. Kousouli's Secret Loving Self Tip #4
GIVE YOURSELF SOME GRACE

I put this at the front of the book knowing that it is probably the hardest tip to incorporate into your life. What do I mean by "giving yourself grace"? I mean allowing yourself the time to heal, showing yourself respect for your attempts to heal and make yourself whole, and not expecting too much too fast – give yourself time. You are who you are *right now*, and the efforts you're making are moving you forward to something great. Be patient, and be gracious to yourself for the efforts you have already made.

So how exactly do you give yourself grace? Forgive all and change your focus.

Dr. Kousouli's Secret Loving Self Tip #5
FOCUS ON YOUR FIRST RELATIONSHIP: YOU

"You yourself, as much as anybody in the entire universe,
deserve your love and affection."
~ Buddha

Many times, people who struggle with self-love and depression look to outside influences to help them feel whole and happy. This may look like trying to resolve issues between you and your parents, or seeking a partner who is really not all that healthy for you - just anything to fill the void you feel so strongly. But this is something you must reverse in order to begin healing.

In order to move forward, you need to shake off the chains that drag you down. Whatever has happened to you, no matter how you feel about it, you must look forward with fresh eyes. If you are always trying to compensate for something you did or didn't do, trying to prove to someone that you are lovable, or trying to get answers, you will never move forward. The past is like quicksand; it wants to keep ahold of you, but you can grab a nearby branch and pull yourself out.

In order to focus on yourself, you <u>really need to focus on your-self</u>. Stop trying to please others. Stop trying to figure out why they do what they do. This is about *you* and what you can do to manifest happiness and wholeness in your life. This also means that, until you can work through your own problems, you don't need to take on the problems of anyone else, or add someone else to your problems. Choose to stay single for a while, especially if you're always in and out of toxic relationships.

I always tell my clients, "You have no business being in a relationship until you learn to love yourself first." I want you to discover your major truths in life, challenge your belief systems, learn about who you are, what you offer the world, what your purpose is on this planet, and what you're here to create. We are all a work in progress, some of us further along than others. However, you cannot fill the cup of another unless yours runneth over first.

It's a universal truth that "Like attracts like," and if your energy isn't whole and happy, whom exactly are you attracting? If you've not first put the work in on yourself, why would anyone you partner with want to work to better themselves? I noticed in my own life that the second I chose to take responsibility for myself, my happiness, and my future, people responded to that by reacting in kind… and miracles unfolded. Once you start improving yourself, your environment improves to reflect the positive changes you've made.

Dr. Kousouli's Secret Loving Self Tip #6
LEARN NEW THINGS FROM PEOPLE AND BOOKS

Someone who loves him or herself is always growing; people who are unhappy are not engaging themselves in different ways. The two things I have found that will help you grow the fastest are the people you meet and the books you read. I recommend finding people who share similar interests with you, whether in business, hobbies, or future goals. There are tons of resources out there for finding people to learn from. Attend empowerment seminars, find support groups, or go to public speaking events at colleges or event halls. Interact with people you see engaging in behaviors and activities you'd like to join in on. This takes some bravery, especially if you've struggled with confidence. The one thing I always try to remember when meeting someone new is that they're just as uncomfortable or shy as I am! But everyone loves it when another person makes contact. It's so exciting!

As for the other half, reading, I recommend that you visit your local library and pick up whatever interests you. Obviously, don't check out 30 books in a day and expect to read them all before they're due back. Pick up a book that involves something you want to get better at. Maybe it's carpentry, maybe it's going green, maybe it's parenting, or even how to make origami. Just pick something. I also recommend finding books that center on something you struggle with; self-confidence, beauty, health, money, etc. Obviously you found this book from my BE A MASTER™ series, but there are so many other great books out there that can influence your life in dramatic ways – and teach you something new. Everyone feels more capable when they're armed with a little bit of knowledge!

People and books are the two best (and least expensive) options for bettering yourself, but there are plenty of other ways to learn something new. Check out *BE A MASTER™ OF SUCCESS,* for more info on networking, confidence, and success in life.

Dr. Kousouli's Secret Loving Self Tip #7
(RE)DISCOVER YOUR TALENTS

Speaking of knowledge, why not take a more hands on approach than just reading or hearing about something? You don't have to go back to college and get a degree in abstract art, but you could take a class at your local community college or recreation center. There are tons of online classes in virtually every subject you can think of! I recommend sitting down, taking a moment to think about a direction you'd like to explore, whether it's a specific hobby, subject, or skill you'd like to cultivate, and then investigate your options.

I also suggest that you think back to when you were a kid, or to a time before you were affected by depression or events that prevented you from living life to the fullest. What things did you enjoy? Was it riding your bike, taking a ceramics class, going fishing, or playing in a sandbox? While it may sound cheesy, reliving your childhood activities can help you get connected to who you really are and can help uncover underdeveloped talents you still have!

Think back to the parable of the talents mentioned earlier, and remember: It's your soul duty to develop your talent(s) and multiply them for everyone's enjoyment. Get back into a neglected hobby from your youth, or that has fallen by the wayside as life got "too busy." Paint, sculpt, draw, landscape, collect art, knit, cook… the options are endless! Maybe you want to learn another language, get certified in CPR, or get your pilot or motorcycle license. You'd be amazed what learning and cultivating new (or old) skills can do to expand your happiness and joy. We all think, "You can't teach an old dog new tricks," but without constant growth we are actually atrophying. Our brain needs the exercise and our confidence gets a major boost when you prove to yourself that you can do something you previously thought you couldn't!

Chapter Four:
Treat Yourself

"To love yourself right now, just as you are, is to give yourself heaven.
Don't wait until you die. If you wait, you die now.
If you love, you live now."
~ Alan Cohen

Taking care of ourselves is one of the things most people struggle with; especially those of us with low self-confidence or who lack a strong concept of self worth. The worst part of our inability to take care of ourselves is that it's the *one thing* we need the most: to show ourselves that we are worthy of love and care. It's a vicious cycle; you don't think you're worth the time, energy, money, or respect that it takes to care for yourself, but then you feel worse because you never take care of yourself! Do yourself a favor, and break the cycle. Go! Spoil yourself!

Dr. Kousouli's Secret Loving Self Tip #8
HAVE A SPA DAY

Nothing makes a man or woman feel more "brand new" than a haircut. Try something new, style it differently – show the world that you feel great! While you're at it, go ahead and get your nails done, get a mani/pedi, a full-body coconut oil massage, a facial…pamper yourself all the way! Even if you struggle with justifying spending money on yourself, tell yourself: "I deserve this, I am beautiful (or handsome), and I am going to enjoy it!" You'll walk out of the salon or spa feeling like a new person. And you are! You *are*, by metaphysical definition, a new person. Pretend that you chose to temporarily live in a parallel reality in the body of someone who now values themselves; those emotions and thoughts will seep into your subconscious, making it your *new* reality.

Dr. Kousouli's Secret Loving Self Tip #9
TRAVEL THE WORLD

One thing I hear from older clients and people "getting up there" in age is that they wish they had traveled more. I know this for certain: You'll never regret going on an adventure. You may wonder if you really deserve a beautiful, amazing vacation when you have so many other things you could be doing right here at home, but that's just when you need to get away the most. Find a great deal, pack, and just go! There are countless last minute flights, cruises, and deals online... No excuses!

Not only do you get much needed time away from whatever you're struggling with in life, but travel has a great way of clearing your mind and putting things into perspective. Even a short weekend getaway at a bed and breakfast in another city is financially feasible for many. Travel somewhere different from where you live. If you live in the U.S., this really isn't hard to do. Go somewhere in Europe, Asia, Africa, South America... Anywhere!

You'll see things you never even imagined, you'll meet amazing people, and you'll experience different cultures for yourself. When you learn about how large the world is, your problems seem just a little smaller; a little more manageable. Bring your wonderful experiences home with you, and know that you can always experience something new somewhere else in the world. Single people, as well as married couples before having children, should travel at least four times a year to experience other cultures, see the world, and expand their life experience. Once the children come into the picture, they will provide ample "busy" time to keep your life occupied.

Dr. Kousouli's Secret Loving Self Tip #10
DIVE INTO NATURE'S BLISS

Reconnecting with nature is also a powerful tool for putting everything into perspective, and it reenergizes your soul enough to jumpstart your healing process. Spend time outside, go to the beach (ocean or lake – it doesn't matter!), walk on the grass barefoot. Leave the phone in your bag or your car, and just go for a walk in nature. Go for a hike, pitch a tent and go camping, etc. We are all creations of Nature, and we must return to Nature for a long overdue re-connection.

When we walk in or explore nature, we're also allowing our energy to be boosted by the natural energy from Earth. Walking barefoot allows your foot chakras and leg channels to uptake this energy, and if you do this enough you can essentially recharge your higher chakras, effectively healing you and promoting self-love. For much more information on this, read *BE A MASTER™ OF PSYCHIC ENERGY*.

Dr. Kousouli's Secret Loving Self Tip #11
GET ADEQUATE VITAMIN D AND SUNSHINE

Did you know that scientists claim we are made of the same elements that comets and stardust are comprised of!? How can we feel happy and fulfilled in mind and body if we do not connect to the laws and energies of our Universe? We seclude ourselves away from other humans, sit at a computer under unnatural, dis-ease-producing fluorescent lightbulbs, getting no life-giving sun rays, and we don't get up much to move our bodies for over eight hours at work. Little human connection, a bad diet, drug and prescription pill toxicity, no exercise, and on top of that, Vitamin D deficiency is on the rise. With all of this combined, we can see we are disconnected to health now more than ever. According to the National Institutes of Health, children without adequate Vitamin D can form a leg-bowing disease called rickets and a weak immune system. Adults can form brittle skeletons and osteoporotic bones with an inability to absorb calcium. Adult bodies need the sun (without sunscreen) to synthesize Vitamin D and activate at least 25 mcg (1000 IU) of Vitamin D. The sun's ultraviolet rays penetrate our skin and convert the skin's natural Vitamin D precursor to a molecule called vitamin D_3, which then metabolically converts through the liver and kidneys into a molecule termed *calcitriol,* which is important for good health. There is no way to adequately compute your needed daily sun exposure, as it varies greatly. However, choose sun exposure according to the latitude and longitude you live at, the time of day, time of year, your skin type, ethnicity, and many other factors. As long as you don't burn, experts say a few minutes a day in the sun without creams and chemical barriers is very healthy, and many who are feeling sad, unhappy, or depressed have been found to have a large deficiency of sunshine and vitamin D synthesis in their lives. Studies, like one presented in Belgium by researchers Dr. Bruce Hollis and Dr. Carol Wagner of the Medical University of South Carolina, showed that there are great benefits with getting adequate Vitamin D. The study on Vitamin D during pregnancy and breastfeeding found: drastic lessening of premature births, birth defects, colds and lung infections, and skin diseases like eczema. That sunshine is calling you!

Plenty of studies have been done on the connections between Vitamin D and mental illness, including depression, seasonal affectation disorder, and even schizophrenia. One study published in *Issues in Mental Health Nursing* found that each research trial that studied the effects of phototherapy (UV lights) and Vitamin D discovered marked improvement in patients' mood. Control groups who didn't receive either UV light therapy or Vitamin D supplements did not experience improvement in their moods. Researchers have yet to understand *why* Vitamin D is so strongly lacking in people with mood disorders and the like, but the connection is obvious. Do yourself a favor, and get a mood boost from the sun! It will help you implement the rest of the self-love tips in this book.

Dr. Kousouli's Secret Loving Self Tip #12
SMILE AND LAUGH A LOT; HAVE FUN

"What people in the world think of you is
really none of your business."
~ Martha Graham

Laughter really is the best medicine out there. Studies have proven that people who smile and laugh more are happier *and* healthier. You've probably heard the saying, "Fake it 'til you make it," and this goes for smiling too. I understand that in your current state, smiling doesn't come easily. Maybe you don't even remember the last time you genuinely smiled. But change that right now. Think of a happy memory, or a funny joke, or something ridiculous you conjure up, like an old man wearing a sombrero who is dancing with an ostrich wearing lipstick. Just smile, even if it's not easy.

According to a number of studies reviewed in 2012 by *Psychology Today* writer, Sarah Stevenson, smiling for as little as 5 minutes triggers dopamine, serotonin, and endorphins. Result? You feel a boost in your mood. Other benefits include relaxed muscles, lower blood pressure, and reduced cortisol (which triggers stress responses in the body). Every cell in your body needs to smile!

When you laugh, amazing things happen; some studies are finding that the body ages differently for people who laugh often. People who were subjects in a study highlighted by *Huffington Post* in 2014 laughed at funny videos once daily for 20 minutes. The control group was told to sit quietly, read, etc. The findings found that people who laughed actually had better memory recall on various memory tasks, their cortisol levels were very low, and they had burned up to 40 calories. Laughter truly does heal!

Still not sold on "faking" a smile or a laugh until it gets more natural? What about how you look when you're smiling or laughing? Many studies cited in the same *Psychology Today* article cited above found that people were more attracted to a person wearing a smile, and felt more at ease approaching a man or woman who was smiling or laughing. Better yet? Smiling and laughter are contagious; you better the day of others when you grace them with your beautiful smile. Look at my goofy smile on the cover of this book, Ha! ☺ Smiling yet? Good! You should be.

Google funny videos to your heart's content, go see a comedian, put in a funny movie, tell a joke – whatever you need to do to get those feel-good juices flowing!

Dr. Kousouli's Secret Loving Self Tip #13
CHERISH YOUR ALONE TIME

"The worst loneliness is to not be comfortable with yourself."
~ Mark Twain

Being alone is not the same as feeling lonely. Being alone with yourself is one of the best ways to cultivate your own opinions, study yourself in different ways, and just *breathe*. So many of us who lack high amounts of self-love feel like being alone is a form of punishment; nobody wants to be around us, why would we want to be alone with us either? This was programmed into our mind from childhood when we were sent to our rooms, given after-school detention, or "time outs"; where being removed from the presence of others was understood as a form of punishment. But instead of running from the discomfort of being alone, embrace it as a blessing. Remember that you are worthy of your own attention and time, and getting comfortable with yourself is one of the best ways to move forward.

Whenever you can, and whenever it's healthy for you, spend time alone. Use it to better yourself and cultivate your mind through the various ways mentioned in this book (books, classes, journaling, and more to come). It's important you take some time every day to spend with yourself. If you have a spouse or children living with you, make sure to make your "alone time" a regular event so that people know not to interrupt.

Once you've focused on putting yourself and your emotional and mental health first, it's time to start thinking about your physical health.

Chapter Five:
Let's Get Physical

"Caring for the mind is as important and crucial as caring for the
body. In fact, one cannot be healthy without the other."
~ Sid Garza-Hillman

You know that working out helps your health, and you probably know that it helps your mental health as well. Even if you feel like you're going to pass out, throw up, or have to ice sore muscles, there's just something about working out that just makes us *feel good.* But thanks to science, we know what that "something" is. Exercise, even a brisk walk or dancing, releases serotonin, dopamine, and nor-epinephrine. Aside from boosting our mood, these chemicals also reverse stress to cells, which can reverse dis-ease and acidosis (more on this in Chapter 6).

Aside from making us feel good, exercise makes us look good, too. As people who struggle with depression and confidence, our appearance is something we constantly get down on ourselves about. Maybe you hate the way you look, maybe you think you're fat, maybe you think you're a hopeless mess. Working out can help you twofold: changing how you *feel* about what you see in the mirror, and changing what you *see* in the mirror. Both are very powerful in reversing negative thoughts of self.

Dr. Kousouli's Secret Loving Self Tip #14
WORKOUT ON A REGULAR BASIS

This goes without saying, but moving your body and respecting it allows you to house a sound mind. The ancient Greeks knew that your body and mind work together; one cannot thrive without the other. If you make a daily effort to honor your body, your mind will benefit as well. You know the physical benefits of exercise, but what about the mental benefits? Studies show that people who exercise at least 5 times a week exhibit fewer signs of depression, anxiety, and negative moods according to the *Journal of Clinical Psychiatry* in 2006.

In addition, people who engage in aerobic (cardiac) exercise have better moods, motivation that translates into other regions of life, and better relationships with themselves and others. For these reasons, I challenge you to start exercising daily, for at least 30 minutes a day for the next 30 days. It doesn't have to be anything huge; just *move* for 30 minutes a day. Work up to more intense activity, and enjoy pushing yourself a little more every day. Make yourself step up, show up, and work out. Get a positive-minded workout buddy if one is available, put on your favorite music and go! Just because you need to exercise doesn't mean it has to be boring!

Dr. Kousouli's Secret Loving Self Tip #15
HAVE FUN WHILE YOU EXERCISE

Nothing ruins an exercise habit faster than getting bored with your workout. Don't go to the gym and run full-speed on a treadmill staring at the wall! Don't do pushups staring at the floor for 15 minutes! Take a minute and think about something physical that you love. It could be something like racquetball or tennis, swimming, or obstacle courses. Find a way to incorporate these activities into your daily or weekly life, and mix it up – make it fun!

Better yet, sign up for a workout class that seems just a tad bit ridiculous. Take a Zumba or Jazzercise class, take a laughing yoga class, or sign up for a costume 5k. Incorporate some fun and humor into your workouts; you get the double benefits of both laughter and exercise. Your brain will be awash in feel-good chemicals, which changes your brain's landscape *and* your body at the same time!

Dr. Kousouli's Secret Loving Self Tip #16
USE THE KOUSOULI® SPINAL STRETCHES FOR
IMPROVED CIRCULATION AND MOOD

One of the best things you'll find for your physical and mental health is a daily routine that supports your inner energies and allows you to set the tone for each part of your day. Many newly-referred clients come to me with postures that reflect their defeated emotions; hunched position (kyphosis), which can also eventually lead to large bends in the length of the spine (scoliosis) causing them to appear shorter, crippled, or even look years older. This feeds into their self-talk; they make themselves smaller and smaller, and their posture tells people all they need to know about them. Other daily activities like sitting, using a computer, or driving also make it hard for us to move our body in ways that honor them. This is why I created the *Kousouli® Spinal Stretches (KSS™)*. It focuses on stretching your spine, getting it in alignment and moving vital chi throughout your body. These simple stretches focus on the center of our bodies, where our chakras are. Aligning these important areas can align other areas of your emotional and physical health.

When we neglect our spines and general posture, we send messages (to ourselves and to others) that we are insecure, unhealthy, and unworthy. That's not the energy you want to radiate out! The *Kousouli® Spinal Stretches (KSS™)* provide a number of benefits for the body, mind, and spirit, which send a message to yourself, other people, and to the universe: "I'm working on myself and am worthy of the best!" A few benefits of the system I have created include:

- Spinae muscle groups become more erect. This improves your posture, making you look and feel better.

- Stretches improve circulation, which improves stamina, awareness, and energy.

- Stretches release tension, which can increase your happiness and confidence.

- Stretches burn calories, making you leaner and fitter.

- Stretches release endorphins, which improve your mood and therefore the energy you exude when meeting life's problems head on.

- Triggers your emotional and confidence centers; aligning the chakras tell your body that you are changing and are capable!

Some notes before you begin:

- Always consult your doctor before beginning any exercise or stretching program like KSS™.

- If you feel pain when performing any movements - stop immediately.

- Begin your KSS™ gently - do not 'jump right in' forcefully. Give yourself time to adapt.

- If you have had a joint replacement or are just coming out of surgery, simply limit, restrict, or avoid major movements.

- KSS™ movements and methods may be modified and adapted to suit an individual's age, needs, and abilities. Do the modified versions labeled 'M' if the original stretch is too difficult for you.

- A KSS™ program for seniors or arthritis sufferers may be applied slowly, and modified gradually over a period of time, depending on skill level. Move your joints slowly through a full range of motion several times, to help enhance overall circulation, and decrease any stiffness. KSS™ may be resumed once tenderness has diminished and your doctor allows you back to total activity.

- Rest painful, inflamed, or hot joints with a cold ice compress at 15-30 minute intervals, and discontinue for the time being if pain occurs.

- Always breathe deeply down into your diaphragm (not chest), and allow unrestricted flow of your airway while doing KSS™ movements.

- Be sure to use a pillow or soft mat for any joints (like the knees) that make constant contact with the ground during modified stretching.

- Practice good technique; do not overextend joints beyond the normal range of motion. Maintain good form and posture.

- Hydrate often throughout the day (A full glass of water per hour awake is recommended.)

- When learning the stretches, consult a more experienced KSS™ user for proper form and execution, rather than learning the poses incorrectly.

- Follow your stretching with a cool-down period, including sustaining the end of the stretch to avoid tenderness or stiffness. If soreness or stiffness occurs despite performing a cool-down, reduce your movements and try the modified 'M' version of the stretch.

Instructions on Kousouli® Spinal Stretches (KSS™)

Beginning your new KSS™ stretching routine is simple! Just pick three stretches (out of the nine provided) to do once in the morning, once in the afternoon, and once in the evening. They can be the same three stretches, but it is recommended that you mix it up in order to get the full advantage of this process. Make sure you that you're paying special attention to your form, and giving these stretches the respect they deserve. They will help change your life!

Please note: each stretch can be modified to your individual abilities! There will be a letter "M" next to suggested changes, but feel free to adapt your own until you become stronger or more adept at the stretches.

Kousouli ® Spinal Stretches (KSS™)

(A.) HERMES STRETCH

To use this morning stretch, start with one arm extended straight up over your shoulder and the knee bent towards your chest. Inhale deeply, and slightly extend your back as you hold the stretch for three seconds. Slowly switch the arms and legs as you exhale. Repeat the stretch on the opposite side. Modified Hermes is done by lying on your back. As you inhale and exhale from your diaphragm, visualize your spiritual body encompassing love for yourself, and feel healing energies coursing through you.

HERMES 1

HERMES 2

HERMES M1

HERMES M2

(B.) POSEIDON STRETCH

To get the best benefits of this stretch, do it in the morning. Crouch on the floor, inhale deeply from your diaphragm, and rise up into a standing position with one leg back while extending the spine and pushing the chest out. Keep your arms wide, and hold up your chin. Hold for three seconds, and then exhale as you come back down into a crouched position. Repeat the stretch with the opposite leg. Use this stretch as a meditation to flush out tensions, resentments, or anything blocking you from loving yourself.

POSEIDON 1   POSEIDON 2   POSEIDON M1   POSEIDON M2

(C.) APHRODITE/EROS STRETCH

I recommend doing this stretch in the morning when you shower, or in a bright sunny spot as you start your day. Stand with your left hand on your trapezius and pull the shoulder muscles down and forward. Anchor your fingers from your right hand onto the left posterior inferior occipital ridge (bottom left edge of skull, see picture: Eros2). Gently pull your head forward, down, and to the right with the chin towards your right chest. Inhale and exhale, feeling the stretch. Repeat on the opposite side (Eros 1). Next, perform a loving heart hug by wrapping your arms around your chest (Eros 3, 4) as you extend your head back. With a gentle squeeze, try to move your fingers as far back to your spine as possible.

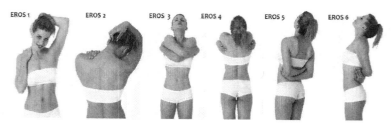

EROS 1   EROS 2   EROS 3   EROS 4   EROS 5   EROS 6

Next, wrap your arms around your low back for support. Extend your upper body back gently, feeling the stretch (Eros 5, 6). The modified version of this stretch can be done seated. Use this stretch as a meditation; use the water flowing over you as a representation of your worthiness, or focus on how blessed you are to feel the sun on your face. Be thankful.

(D.) APOLLO STRETCH

This stretch is a great stretch to engage your muscles during the afternoon. Start in a standing position, inhale deeply from your diaphragm, arch your spine, and push out your chest as you pull one arm and leg back. Put yourself into an archer position, and hold for a three second count. Exhale as you come back to starting position. Focus on the fluid motion of your body as tension builds upon extension of the back and arms. Repeat on the opposite side. Modify this stretch by kneeling or sitting with legs crossed. Use this as a meditation; aim your arrow and shoot for what you want in life and for yourself.

APOLLO 1   APOLLO 2   APOLLO M1   APOLLO M2

(E.) HEPHAESTUS STRETCH

This is a great mid-day stretch to get your body moving after a long day behind a desk. To do the Hephaestus stretch, move from an extended standing position to a crouched forward pose, as if you were wielding a large axe or hammer to the ground. Inhale as you slowly extend a leg and stretch back, hold for three seconds, and then come down gently forward overhead, bending the knees as you exhale. Rotate slightly your upper body through the movement to isolate the abdominals. Go slow and do not overextend your back. Repeat the stretch on the opposite side. Modified version is done by kneeling or sitting with legs crossed. Use this stretch to symbolize your efforts to work on yourself, and overcome your demons. When you extend your arms, you can witness your work being transferred into abundance and self-love.

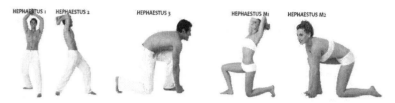

(F.) ATHENA STRETCH

Stand with flexed biceps as if you are holding a large shield in each arm. Extend your spine slightly and inhale deeply. Turn your arms and upper torso to one side and bring up the opposite knee. Tighten your abdominal muscles and hold for three seconds. Exhale and repeat on the other side. As you breathe deep from your diaphragm, perceive yourself as an impenetrable fortress. Use this as a time to reflect on who you are. Outside forces do not influence you, and are deflected off your energy's armor.

(G.) ZEUS STRETCH

The stretch should be started with your body crouched and then slowly extend your arms up as you stand into a body X position. Inhale deeply as you slowly stretch to the sky, pushing up on your toes.

Feel the stretch as you hold for three seconds. Exhale slowly as you descend back into a crouched position. As you descend and exhale, cross your arms as if throwing lightning bolts down to earth from the heavens. Repeat. Focus on the slow fluid motion of your body as tension builds up on the upward motion, and then releases on the downward flow. Modified Zeus stretch can be done kneeling or sitting with legs crossed. Use your downward motion with breathing to let go of any stress you accumulated during your day. Envision any negative energy slide off and be thrown to the ground. Enter a clear space where you can bring higher vibrations of energy to your self-improvement efforts.

ZEUS 1   ZEUS 2   ZEUS 3   ZEUS M1   ZEUS M2

(H.) DIONYSUS STRETCH

Slowly bring up both arms as if holding an oversized glass of wine. Inhale deeply from your diaphragm, and slowly extend your torso as you rotate to one side. Gently extend your neck and upper back as if you are drinking the wine. Hold for three seconds, and keep your core tight. Return to center as you exhale, and then repeat on the opposite side. Use this stretch to celebrate your vitality and love for living life as only you can.

DIONYSUS 1   DIONYSUS 2   DIONYSUS M1   DIONYSUS M2

(I.) DEMETER STRETCH

The Demeter stretch is best done at night, and allows us to truly focus on how many cycles we experience. Lie on your back and inhale as you squeeze your knees to your chest; this signifies new life. Hold for three seconds, and then exhale as you slowly extend your legs down; depicting the seasonal summer/winter cycles. At the completion, slightly arch your cervical (neck) and the lumbar area (low back). Repeat. The modified version is done with hands palm-down under the low back or hips for support, and makes the stretch a little easier. Use this stretch to symbolize your day as a cycle; tomorrow begins anew. Your confidence and emotions also cycle, and may wax and wane, stretch and contract. Remember that everything starts new when the cycle begins again.

DEMETER 1

DEMETER 2

DEMETER M1

DEMETER M2

Benefits to the KSS™ Stretch Program

KSS™ combines a very unique mix of visual meditation, deep breathing, and spinal exercise to provide an extremely powerful physical, mental, and spiritual release. Not only will these stretches become easier as you progress, but you will also come to rely on them to start your day, jumpstart your energy levels in the afternoon, and prepare yourself for bed. KSS™ allows you to focus on intentions and positive thoughts, which allows you a clear headspace before you can approach your life with positivity. When the mind, body, and spirit work together as they do in these exercises, you will not only feel and look better, but you will exude light and love for yourself.

Dr. Kousouli's Secret Loving Self Tip #17
GET ADEQUATE SLEEP

I often tell my clients that sleep is one of the most underrated tools for healing and self-improvement. While we wear our minimal sleep hours like a badge on our chests ("Oh yeah, well I only got *three* hours of sleep last night!"), our bodies are taking huge hits to emotional and physical repair centers. Sleep triggers hormone responses in the brain that go to work to repair damage to the body, and also develop connections to parts of the brain that have been exhausted.

Have you ever had a day where you were so emotionally drained that you felt beyond exhausted, even though you hadn't done anything physical? Your brain needs to reboot so that your emotions can, too! But use this tool with caution. Many people with depression are prone to sleeping long hours every day, experiencing listlessness and lethargy, and prevent themselves from accomplishing anything because they just feel "so tired." In this case, the issue may be an overloaded, toxic body that needs a doctor's analysis and care. Get the recommended amount of sleep for your body (usually between 7-9 hours), and work out in the mornings to wake yourself up and feel great.

If you'd like to dip into how sleep along with dieting, and working out affect your body and self-esteem, check out my other book, *BE A MASTER™ OF SELF IMAGE.*

Chapter Six:
Enlist the Help of Professionals

"We hold life to be precious at birth and death, yet sometimes forget the beautiful parts in between."
~ Dr. Theo Kousouli

Sometimes, no matter how hard we try, we just can't do this thing alone. For some of us, this is a really hard thing to admit: that we need help in filling in the gaps to that which we don't know how to do ourselves. But there is strength in admitting our vulnerability, and there is power in asking for help. It shows that you're not giving up, that you're using every tool you have in your arsenal to overcome the "demons" (or negative thought vibrations) that keep trying to drag you down.

Dr. Kousouli's Secret Loving Self Tip #18
SEEK PROFESSIONAL HELP

Many people think of sitting on a couch and talking about their parents when they consider going to see a hypnotherapist, counselor, psychologist, or psychiatrist. In reality, it's a little bit like that – but quite a bit different, too. You sit down and you talk through what's bothering you, and there is enormous power in that single act. Talking it out is very valuable when you feel you've given it all with your friends and family, but you're not getting anywhere. You feel less guilty and more productive when you're talking to someone who has been through what you've been through, or is an expert in your specific needs.

I recommend that you seek support groups, whether it's abuse survivor groups, depression or mental health, or whatever you personally need "in-person" that can help you get the clarity you seek. If you are at a loss on how to find resources and support groups, here are a few national hotlines that can give you immediate support, as well as resources. You must take decisive action! Just call them; they can really help!

- The National Suicide Prevention Lifeline: Call 1-800-273-TALK (8255) or call 911 immediately

- The Substance Abuse and Mental Health Services Administration: Call 1-800-662-HELP

- Depression and Bipolar Support Assistance: Call 1-800-826-3632

- Mental Health America (can provide referrals to professionals and support groups): Call 1-800-950-NMHA (6642)

- National Domestic Violence Hotline: Call 1-800-799-SAFE (7233)

- National Sexual Assault Hotline: Call 1-800-656-HOPE (4763)

You can also research support in your area by getting online or checking a phonebook for mental health services, or you can ask for support from your local place of worship, school, or human resources department. The worst part about depression and emotional struggle is that you feel entirely alone. I hope you know that you are not alone; all you have to do is reach out and ask for help. There are many systems of support available to you.

Once you've reached out to a professional for mental support, you'll be able to find a holistic health professional or system that can help you address other concerns. Using professional advice is one of the best ways to streamline your success; you can see results faster when you finally accept help from others and take advice from others who have come before you with similar struggles!

Dr. Kousouli's Secret Loving Self Tip #19
USE THE 4R KOUSOULI® METHOD INTERVENTION SYSTEM

My experience with the different aspects of chiropractic care, clinical research, energy healing, clairvoyant meditation, hypnosis, and personal experiences in and out of the clinic - both as a doctor and as a patient - have helped me develop the Kousouli® Method 4R Intervention System of Health. **The main goal of the Kousouli® Method is to treat the patient by addressing vital energy loss in 4 main arenas (spiritual, mental, emotional, and physical) utilizing the 'antenna' called the nervous system.** The nervous system allows us to interact with our internal and external environments and is the master communicator of our health. The Kousouli® Method 4R Intervention System gives patients a daily checklist and simple structure for making sure they are on point to "Rejuvenate the Body, Empower the Mind, and Free the Soul." When we enter states of sadness, depression, or severe emotional struggles, we enter a dis-ease state that can affect every other region of our health and lives.

The diagrams on the next few pages show the cycles of positivity, negativity, and what happens when you utilize the 4R system. In the first cycle, we see where most people are when they feel something is wrong or feel ill. Because of accumulated negative experiences or neglect over time, people feel lousy and seek out mental or spiritual aid to help them recover from their depression. Once you implement the steps in this system, you will begin to return to a positive energy state. If a person maintains the 4R system, the patient will stay in this positive cycle until neglect over time pulls the process back to the negative cycle. **The success of the method is due to the focus on the** *4R continuous processes*:

1. *Remove the* **toxins.** Cautiously limit or remove (as much as possible with doctor supervision) all drug use (prescription, over-the-counter, or recreational), alcohol consumption, caffeine, sodas, smoking, intestinal worms & parasites, heavy metal toxicity, allergens, electro-magnetic radiation, old scar tissue build-up, junk food and fast food, environmental and occupational ergonomic hazards.

2. *Revive* **the nervous system utilizing correct chiropractic care.** Chiropractic adjustments reduce spinal stress and open vital communication pathways from the brain to every cell, tissue, and organ in the body.

3. *Rebuild* **the body through whole food nutrition and exercise.** Proper hydration, nourishment, oxygenation, supplementation, exercise, stretching, and deep tissue re-organization of spinal muscle attachments.

4. *Reset* **your thoughts and programming.** Prayer, meditation, visualization, hypnotic suggestion, Kousouli® Neural Emotive Reconditioning (KNER™), and proper mind and body rest will ensure that the whole process is perpetuated within yourself, and that you continue to reap the benefits for the rest of your life.

Going through the Kousouli® Method 4R intervention system will ensure you get the 5th 'R' too; *Recovery!* My simple message is: those who love themselves and have moved forward from their pasts make daily progress and strive for persistent positive states. Don't lie to yourself thinking that just popping some anti-depression pills and going to see a counselor once is going to fix you. To stay in the positive cycle, without losing any progress by relapse, you *must* decide your happiness and life are priorities worth maintaining over the course of your life - not just for a week or a few months. The 4R Kousouli® Method Intervention System now makes it much easier to keep yourself on track and move towards fully loving yourself.

Those with healthy lives make daily healthy choices. Adding the steps of *Remove, Revive, Rebuild, and Reset* into your life *over time* will help you *regain health.*

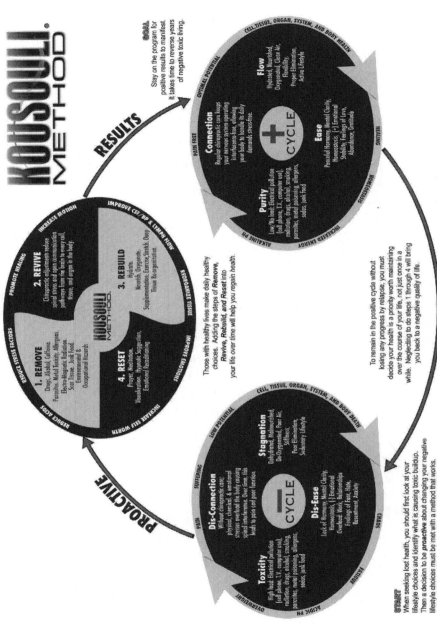

KOUSOULI METHOD®

RESULTS
Stay on the program for positive results to manifest. It takes time to reverse years of negative toxic living.

1. REMOVE
Drugs, Alcohol, Caffeine, Parasites, Metal Toxicity, Allergies, Electro-Magnetic Radiation, Scar Tissue, Junk Food, Environmental & Occupational Hazards.

2. REVIVE
Chiropractic adjustments reduce spinal stress and open communication pathways from the brain to every cell, tissue, and organ in the body.

3. REBUILD
Hydrate, Nourish, Oxygenate, Supplementation, Exercise, Stretch, Deep Tissue Re-organization.

4. RESET
Proper, Nutrition, Visualization, Hypnotic Suggestion, Emotional Reconditioning.

Those with healthy lives make daily healthy choices. Adding the steps of *Remove, Revive, Rebuild, and Reset* into your life over time will help you *regain health.*

REDUCE STRESS FACTORS · PROMOTE HEALING · INCREASE MOTION · IMPROVE CSF, BP & LYMPH FLOW · IMPROVE CSF/BP & LYMPH FLOW · REORGANIZE TISSUE · IMPROVE EMOTIONS · INCREASE SELF WORTH · REDUCE ACIDS

+ CYCLE
OPTIMAL POTENTIAL · CELL, TISSUE, ORGAN, SYSTEM, AND BODY HEALTH · HEALING

Connection
Regular chiropractic care keeps your nervous system operating interference-free, allowing your body to handle its daily demands stress-free.

Flow
Hydrated, Nourished, Oxygenated, Clean Air, Flexibility, Proper Elimination, Active Lifestyle

Ease
Peaceful Harmony, Mental Clarity, Homeostasis, (+) Emotional Stability, Feelings of Love, Abundance, Gratitude

Purity
Low/No level Electrical pollution (cell phone, T.V., computer use), radiation, drugs, alcohol, smoking, parasites, metal poisoning, allergies, sodas, junk food

PAIN FREE · HOMEOSTASIS · INCREASED ENERGY · ALKALINE PH

To remain in the positive cycle without losing any progress by relapse, you must decide your health is a priority worth maintaining over the course of your life, not just once in a while. Neglecting to do steps 1 through 4 will bring you back to a negative quality of life.

NEGLECT

PROACTIVE

SUFFERING · PAIN · FATIGUE · OVERWEIGHT · ACIDIC PH · TIRED

- CYCLE
LOW POTENTIAL · CELL, TISSUE, ORGAN, SYSTEM, AND BODY DEATH · ALKALINE PH

Dis-Connection
Without chiropractic care; physical, chemical & emotional stresses overload the body causing spinal interference. Over time this leads to pain and poor function.

Stagnation
Dehydrated, Malnourished, De-Oxygenated, Poor Air, Stiffness, Poor Elimination, Sedentary Lifestyle

Dis-Ease
Lack of Harmony, Mental Clarity, Homeostasis, (-) Emotional Overload Worry, Relationships, Feelings of Fear, Hate, Resentment, Anxiety

Toxicity
High level Electrical pollution (cell phone, T.V., computer use), radiation, drugs, alcohol, smoking, parasites, metal poisoning, allergies, sodas, junk food

START
When seeking lost health, you should first look at your lifestyle choices and identify what is causing toxic buildup. Then a decision to be *proactive* about changing your negative lifestyle choices must be met with a method that works.

Staying in the Positive Cycle

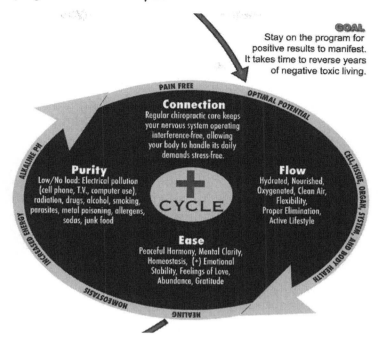

Connection: Regular chiropractic care keeps your nervous system operating in an interference-free fashion, allowing your body to handle its daily demands in a stress-free manner.

Flow: Incorporating proper hydration, nourishment, oxygen, clean air, flexibility, proper elimination, and an active lifestyle will ensure a smooth flow of positive energy within your body.

Ease: Having peaceful purpose, harmony, mental clarity, homeostasis, positive emotional stability, feelings of love, abundance, and gratitude for yourself and others will keep you in a positive frame of mind.

Purity: Avoid or remove electrical pollution (cellular phone, televisions, and computers), radiation, drugs, alcohol, smoking, parasites, metal poisoning, allergens, sodas, caffeine overload, junk, or fast food.

Reverting Back to the Negative Cycle Through Neglect

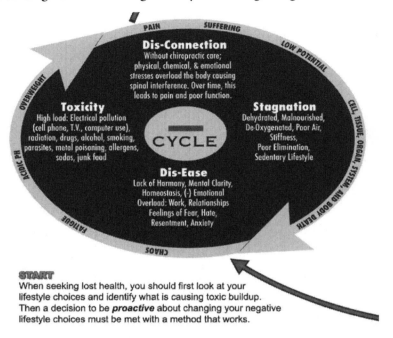

START
When seeking lost health, you should first look at your lifestyle choices and identify what is causing toxic buildup. Then a decision to be **proactive** about changing your negative lifestyle choices must be met with a method that works.

Dis-connection: Irregular, discontinuous, or complete lack of chiropractic care; physical, chemical, and emotional stresses all compound spinal overload. Over time, this miscommunication of brain-to-body leads to pain and poor function.

Stagnation: Staying in a dehydrated condition, receiving improper nutrition, no or low supplementation, poor air or water quality, lymph flow backup, poor elimination, and a sedentary lifestyle are big ways to bring your health down.

Dis-Ease: Lack of harmony, mental clarity, negative emotional stresses, work or relationship stress overload, feelings of fear, hate, resentment, anxiety, or self-loathing all will contribute to dis-ease conditions.

Toxicity: High load of electro-magnetic pollution, radiation, drugs, alcohol, smoking, parasites, heavy metal poisoning, allergens, sodas, and junk food will result in an overall imbalance and a downslide of your health condition. Also consider emotional toxicity and the relationships around you that need to be evaluated for their "health conditions."

It becomes apparent from the above points that most of your health is a matter of lifestyle choice; some mental or physical pre-dispositions cannot be helped, but we have control over how much they affect us. Consistency is key in maintaining a healthy condition, and the more consistent you are with your good habits and lifestyle choices, the better you will be served by your mind and body. This system is a great guide for keeping yourself in check; refer to it often to ensure you are doing all 4 aspects adequately enough to maintain your homeostatic balance. It will help remind you if you've been skipping or neglecting yourself by thinking negative thoughts, engaging in poor eating behaviors, not staying hydrated, or missing your last chiropractic appointment - all of which would start leaning you towards the negative cycle.

The Kousouli® Method 4R Intervention System is continuously being adapted through clinical application and research. When correctly applied, it has shown successful symptom reduction or elimination of headaches, dizziness, fatigue/low energy, carpel tunnel, whiplash pains, muscle spasms, joint pains, neck pain, back pain, allergies, depression, hormonal imbalances, fibromyalgia, numbness, limb tingling, IBS, asthma, acid reflux/GERD, arthritis, insomnia, and toxicity - just to name a few. The Kousouli® Method through KNER™ also takes into account the spiritual, mental, and emotional aspects of health, which usually manifest into the physical plane as pain and dis-ease. By accessing specific chakra and spinal energy points, and balancing these points, the individual can focus their energy on healing with quicker results. Your brain, body, mind, and spirit are entirely connected, so use this method to help you address your past and current struggles by thoroughly caring for yourself.

This system's powerful technique of replenishing health naturally goes beyond the scope of this book and is taught privately to interested practitioners at live seminar events. Details can be found at www.Kousouli-Method.com.

Acidosis and Depression

I would like to further drive home the point that the way you feel in your mind is not isolated to just your mind; it's affecting your body as well. As I noted in my book, *BE A MASTER™ OF MAXIMUM HEALING*, any health issue that brings the body out of homeostasis must be looked at as a whole body issue, not just as a "single" issue. Depression, suicide attempts, mood swings, insomnia, anxiety, etc. are all effects of a deeper-seated issue. When people feel pain (emotional or physical), or are distressed or grieving, they are exhibiting a manifestation of the negative cycle. A patient in less than optimum states is most likely starting, or already in, the process called the 'acid state.' You need to understand the basics of acidosis, as it is the root cause of all dis-ease afflicting us as humans. Our bodies work under a finely regulated homeostatic balance of acids and bases (a.k.a. alkalis) 24/7, 365 days a year. The body also produces its own neutralizing buffers to keep the overall acidity under control. But when our mental and emotional states prevent overall alkalinity, our body enters a state of acidosis, which leads to dis-ease and continuation of the negative cycle. Basically, you can't get out of your rut because your body is stuck in it now, too.

Every organ in your body is affected by your mental and spiritual state of negativity. When you alter the alkalinity of your body, you're affecting your: colon (which cannot properly flush your body's excrement), heart (which cannot properly oxygenate), stomach (which cannot digest food properly, resulting in the stomach pain you feel every time you enter a negative or depressed state), and more. Your liver, kidneys, pancreas, and lymphatic system enter a state of crisis; they can't filter your body's waste like they usually do, nor react to threats (viruses and bad bacteria). It's like anarchy in your brain and your body. No wonder you feel bad!

How Negative Energy Contributes to Acidosis

You might be thinking, "There's no way my past abuse/bad relationship/negative self image has any effect on my health." But I'm here to tell that any kind of negative emotion can use up reserve energy, tax body function, increase free radicals, and create acidity. An increase in stress beyond normal amounts will lead to acidosis. Have you ever said, "I am sick to my stomach" or heard, "Your problems are eating away at your happiness"? These are emotional states, which make you highly prone to acidosis and set the stage for dis-ease. I recommend that you choose to only talk to yourself like your best friend would; only say good things and throw away the thoughts of fear and anger. Choose the path of love for yourself. Yes, it is a choice; your choice.

Chapter Seven:
Choosing Holistic Health for Body and Mind

"To go from a light bulb to a lighthouse, the old soul must heal its repressed lack of self-love."
~ Dr. Theo Kousouli

In the previous chapter, we discussed the need for professional help and whole body systems that can help your body and mind reach new heights. But maybe you're wondering how in the world you're going to change your mind and love yourself when you can't even figure out how to eat better. Here are my tips for setting your body into the positive cycle by *Removing* waste, detoxifying your body, and *Rebuilding* the body with better ingredients.

Dr. Kousouli's Secret Loving Self Tip #20
EAT AND DRINK ONLY WHAT IS NATURAL

For most of us, the thought of cutting out our creature comforts is a fate worse than death – or so we think. But have you actually tried it? When you're sad or feeling terrible about yourself, what's the first thing you do? Cancel all your plans and grab a box of cookies, right? This behavior of negative looping is natural to humans, and obviously you're not the only person out there who connects emotions to food. But I'm telling you right now that you can change this habit, and you can create a new one where you fuel your body with the foods that will *heal* you, inside and out, and give you a new lease on life. I recommend that you:

1.   **Eat your greens.** Maintain a chlorophyll-rich, plant-based, clean diet with very light meats (chicken, turkey, salmon)

and eat the majority of your daily food in the form of vegetables or plants of some sort.

2. **Drink water, and remove sugars and artificial drinks.** Keeping hydrated allows acids to flow out easier and maintains normal blood pH and viscosity. Phosphoric acid is in all sodas and wreaks havoc in your body. Instead, load up on green drinks that contain chlorophyll, or cold-pressed, fresh fruit juices that don't have added sugar.

3. **Detoxify your digestive system.** Constipation or diarrhea can both throw your electrolyte balance off track and make you feel sick. The colon can also accumulate toxins if improper bowel movements become a norm. Therefore, the first part of any effective corrective program is toxin removal through digestive tract cleansing. Colon hydrotherapy, psyllium, home enemas, and herbal colon cleansers that incorporate a combination of internal cleansing herbs are all part of an ideal detoxification program.

4. **Remove heavy metals and toxins.** See a holistic nutritionist and doctor of functional medicine for toxic heavy metal removal (a sluggish or repressed system could be connected to a thyroid condition). Check for leaky gut syndrome, candida albicans (yeast syndrome) overgrowth, and celiac disease (gluten intolerance). Do a liver, gallbladder, colon, and parasite cleanse if you can. You can also try chelation therapy to remove all heavy metals, further lightening the load on your circulatory system.

5. **Remove toxic medicines and poor foods/alcohol from your diet.** Talk to your doctor about removing medications from your daily diet, and set up a time schedule for weaning or reducing. Also remember that the body will go

through withdrawal symptoms, especially if the patient is addicted to high glycemic carbohydrates, diet and caffeine drinks, smoking or drinking. Patients will usually experience issues like: fever, nausea, headaches, chills, ulcers, skin rashes, thirst, increased urination, loss of appetite, eye pain, difficulty sleeping, extreme drowsiness and fatigue, diarrhea, muscle soreness, lack of motivation, and any already known problems usually become heightened briefly. This detox side effect phenomenon is termed a 'healing crisis' and generally lasts for a 1 to 2 week period (or longer) after starting a detox. This is a good thing - even if it feels like it's the exact opposite!

Depression and Diet

Depression and negative states of energy have become a real problem in the world we live in. Depression and other mental disorders result in 41,000+ deaths by suicide every year, according to the National Institute of Mental Health. We should never forget that our mental state is a direct reflection of internal nutritional status, our overall lifestyle quality, and our thought process in general. This is why I so strongly recommend detoxifying yourself and fixing your biochemical status, using exercise programs to refocus yourself and divert attention from origins of negative energy, and seek spinal realignment through the Kousouli® Method 4R Intervention System of Health to reduce toxic stress loads.

In no time, you'll see how choosing what you put into your body, expecting more from your body, and focusing on making your body better will help you solve so many of the spiritual and mental energy struggles you have. In the next chapter, we will focus on tools for spiritual healing. If you want to learn even more, read *BE A MASTER™ OF PSYCHIC ENERGY* to learn how to use your personal energy for more spiritual empowerment.

Chapter Eight:
Spiritual Healing

"And God said, Let us make man in our image, after our likeness:
and let them have dominion over the fish of the sea, and over the
fowl of the air, and over the cattle, and over all the earth, and
over every creeping thing that creepeth upon the earth."
~ Genesis 1:26

Given that you picked up this book to learn how to love yourself, you've probably been expecting this section to pop up sooner than it is. Why address spiritual healing so late in the book? Because I want people to understand that there are many other aspects of our daily lives that affect our ability to heal. You can't grab all the puzzle pieces, sit down, and expect all of the pieces to fit together in just a few minutes. You have to find the edge pieces, work your way into the middle (the spirit) of the puzzle, and then you can finally find that last piece you've been struggling to find this whole time.

Because you've already done so much self-development and worked hard on improving your conscious mind and physical body, I am now going to recommend that you keep improving your other higher mind; your intuitive "master" mind.

Dr. Kousouli's Secret Loving Self Tip #21
MEDITATE AND PRAY DAILY

For many people who are new to self-help and improvement world, the idea of meditation seems "hokey" or like something "regular people" with "regular problems" just don't do. That's incredibly far from the truth. Take five minutes to think about or research successful happy people who meditate daily; odds are someone you love dearly or know well also meditates. Once you make this connection, you'll realize you don't have to be a Zen monk to pull it off.

The world, and your place within it, must make sense to you in order to find your peace. Meditation and prayer can do that for you. So what is meditation, exactly, and how can it benefit your inner struggles to love yourself? Meditation is basically *mindful awareness* – you are sitting with yourself, your thoughts, and your bodily sensations and breathing through all of the things that pop into your brain; stripping the mind of all distraction, focusing on bringing peace and tranquility to you, and just *being*.

Prayer is different; prayer is creating in your space through a state of gratitude and connection with the divine. Try out and explore Christ Consciousness through Christian meditation (as opposed to Transcendental meditation explained above). In original Christianity, the true message was and still is love, not malicious religious dogma. Prayer can simply take the form of you asking for something and being in the relaxed space to receive (create/manifest) it.

In both cases, you focus on just being in order to send or receive positive energy. Remember: You can try to clear your mind of every thought, but they're going to pop up. Your ear is going to itch. Your dog is going to bark. But the idea is that you notice those things and go back to thinking about your breathing. This is over-simplifying quite a bit, but for the purpose of brevity I want to keep it simple.

How to Meditate and Pray

I recommend sitting quietly in an isolated area of your house first thing in the morning or right before bed for five minutes. Sit on a chair, on a pillow on the floor, or just on the floor if needed. Play around with whatever position feels comfortable, and just breathe. Five minutes will feel like forever for the first few times, but then you'll naturally grow your "meditation muscle" and can build up to longer and better sessions. Meditation benefits people who struggle with depression, self love, and who want to overcome their pasts because it teaches them to live in the moment, rather than in the past, or the future. There is only the present! Eventually when you become great at it, you will learn to meditate throughout the day, as a 365, 24/7 activity as it flows into a normal routine. You won't have to set aside time for meditation as a separate activity. Once in this place of mind tranquility, you will be able to pray by simply asking for (and being open to receiving) anything you wish. For much more detailed explanation on the processes of meditation and prayer, read *BE A MASTER™ OF PSYCHIC ENERGY.*

Dr. Kousouli's Secret Loving Self Tip #22
KEEP A SPIRITUAL DEVELOPMENT NOTEBOOK

With meditation, I find that journaling, or keeping a notebook of your thoughts, helps to really clear your mind and allow you to be present with your ideas. As you grow, you will have experiences, dreams, ideas, thoughts of divine genius; write them all down! You must not let them fade away once you have these intuitive flashes of wisdom, so it is important you transfer the idea to the written word as soon as possible. One of the best parts of meditating is that you have these little (or huge) realizations about yourself, about life, and about your past or future.

When you write things down, you're essentially signaling to your brain that you're processing through a problem, making movements towards a specific end result. This also signals to the Universe that you're making moves to improve yourself, and have even made huge breakthroughs! Write it down, and focus all your energy into continually improving yourself through meditation. Who knows – maybe your meditation will bring you a fantastic idea, just like mine brought me to writing this book for you!

Chapter Nine:
Relationships - Pull the Weeds and Grow the Flowers

"No one can make you feel inferior without your consent."
~ *Eleanor Roosevelt*

Now that you've worked on all of your internal factors that influence depression, confidence, and self-love, let's take a minute to evaluate the external influences that can make or break your progress. Let's be honest: someone else's mistakes, or your interpretation of someone else's behavior has caused the imbalance you're struggling to correct. Why in the world would you want to work so hard on bettering yourself, only to have the same toxic and abusive people surrounding you? But for most of us, the same people that we have allowed to get us to where we are (in this hole of depression and self-loathing) are our closest family and friends. So what do we do?

Dr. Kousouli's Secret Loving Self Tip #23
SET UP AND RESPECT YOUR PERSONAL BOUNDARIES

This is quite possibly one of the most important steps in this book. Even if the people you are surrounded by aren't the ones who have affected your programming, abused you, or fed into your cycle of negativity, you have to be able to distance yourself from their individual issues. You must know when to say no, and when to let go of those who are disrespecting your personal space and time. If you're too nice, this is a problem. You can be cool, awesome, sweet, loving, amazing...but don't be "nice." "Nice" tends to get run over and taken advantage of; especially in the areas of love and relationships. Grow a thicker skin, and get those boundaries set up. You cannot please everyone, and you shouldn't want to try. For example, if you have a poor relationship with your father that feeds into your own cycle of negativity, you may need to set up boundaries that prevent situations from arising. Some people may choose to limit contact except for family events and holidays, or have certain "no-go" topics like politics or religion that fire up the issues they have with their father. For other people, this may look like telling that one friend who drains your energy (an energy vampire) that, no, you really can't let them live with you for free for a month while they get on their feet.

"Don't sacrifice yourself too much, because if you sacrifice too much there's nothing else you can give and nobody will care for you."
~ Karl Lagerfeld

One thing to keep in mind with this step is that their negativity will always try to guilt you into sticking around and continuing the cycle of negativity you perpetuate together. Stick to your guns; eventually they will realize that you're not budging, and they'll stop pushing. For more information on the importance of removing energy vampires, check out *BE A MASTER™ OF SUCCESS and BE A MASTER™ OF PSYCHIC ENERGY.*

Dr. Kousouli's Secret Loving Self Tip #24
SPEND QUALITY TIME WITH POSITIVE
FRIENDS AND FAMILY

You might be reading that tip and thinking, "But Dr. Kousouli, how am I supposed to know if these people that I should surround myself with are actually positive people?" Everyone puts a good foot forward when they're meeting you for the first time, or when the whole family gets together. This is the hardest part; when you realize that someone is not at all the person you thought they were. To avoid this, I recommend this little tip: Interview your friends, siblings, parents, and grandparents. Make a list of things you want to know and tell them to respond honestly, as if you weren't a relative or friend, but someone who was looking to gain wisdom or insight.

Some questions could be, "Do they think of a cup as half full or half empty?" "Do they dwell on the past or the future?" "What do they do when they've had a bad day?" and so on. Now that you've been working on yourself for so long, you're going to be able to pinpoint exactly those questions and answers that indicate someone isn't as positive as you once thought. "Time" is usually your best friend when determining if someone is showing you their "real" self. Three to nine months is a good evaluation period for checking character consistency. Don't get caught up in trying to help these people. Right now your only concern is helping "numero uno" get clear on what energy and what kinds of programming you allow around you. Make sure you're in a safe place before you try to help others. This goes for self-improvement, especially when it comes to your energy. It is imperative you surround yourself with those who are of positive love and compassion; the more positive loving souls, the merrier. Think about the effect one energy vampire could have on your newly expanded positive energy. It's not going to be constructive. Be picky, and don't "hire" anyone into your space as your positivity co-pilots unless they prove they are a pleasant person to be around.

Chapter Ten:
Self-talk to Grow Self-love

"Wanting to be someone else is a waste of the person you are."
~ Marilyn Monroe

Now that you've selected the people in your inner sanctum, you've established boundaries, and you know exactly what sort of energy you want to let in, you should focus on what sort of energy you're putting out and keeping in yourself. What does this mean? Think about how you talk to yourself. I often tell my clients to think about what they would say to their best friend or sibling when they seek advice or need to vent about a similar issue.

"Would you say this to your best friend?" If the answer is yes, then it can be said. If you wouldn't even say it to your worst enemy, then why in the world do you say it to yourself? So many of us talk to ourselves in a low vibratory way that reflects our true emotions and beliefs about ourselves. Our self-talk is hateful, rather than full of love. So filter everything you say to yourself with the "best friend filter," and focus on changing your inner dialogue. You want to keep your inner and outer energy positive. Here are a few tips to help.

Dr. Kousouli's Secret Loving Self Tip #25
RELEASE YOUR STORY

Stop the "Woe is me" tale of misery you may be spinning in your own head and in conversations with others day in and day out. Everyone has a story; you're not a unique snowflake in that regard. We tend to want special attention by pouting and playing the world's tiniest violin. Stop it! In all honesty, no one cares about your pity party because everyone else is also going through some sort of personal trauma or catastrophe! Some are raped, others are going through major drug addictions, others are orphans, some are handicapped, others off at war… Literally everyone has a story, so stop trying to get others to feel sorry for you.

When you finally step up and say, "This is who I am, but I am not what has happened to me," you free yourself from that old set storyline. Take the pen back, and write your new story moving forward. It's <u>how</u> you deal with your story that makes you a hero or a zero. Let go of the drama, the pain, the despair and live the dream. It's much better on this side, I can promise you that.

Dr. Kousouli's Secret Loving Self Tip #26
DO NOT LIE TO YOURSELF

The ultimate validation of self-love is to honor and feel what your body is telling you it needs, and listening to your intuition. When you call yourself a victim, or think you're not worthy, you're lying to yourself. When you think, "Oh, I can't do this, I'm too stupid," you're lying to yourself and preventing yourself from growing. Your inner "higher self" knows you are able to overcome, thus those statements and any statement of lack mentality is essentially, a lie.

When dealing with yourself, you must always exercise unconditional self-love. Medical hypnotherapist and author of "Home at the Tree of Life" Dr. Elena Gabor agrees:

> "Self-unconditional love is an essential ingredient in experiencing a healthy happy and beautiful life. Self-love leads to unity of consciousness, self-criticism and negative self-talk lead to conflict between the levels of our consciousness, disconnection from our true self, and invites pain and suffering. Self-criticism is the result of forgetting who we truly are and

leads to devaluation of the self. It is a self-destructive attitude.

Love is the most powerful energy that exists, is the fabric of creation, the energy that brings both matter and energy into existence, and through self-criticism one positions him/ herself in conflict with this infinite power. Through self-love one can realign with the higher levels of consciousness, and anchor into the infinite creative power that underlines all levels of existence. Self-love leads to healing. Love heals everything, which leads to experiencing a happy life in integrity with the true self."

Dr. Kousouli's Secret Loving Self Tip #27
BURY THE HATCHET; FORGIVE ALL

Ah! The sweet, sweet feeling of letting go! Possibly the biggest thing that leads to depression, anger, anxiety, acidosis, and dis-ease in the body is holding grudges against yourself or others. If you're prone to holding people's past behaviors against them, you're holding grudges. If you frequently say things like, "I can't believe I did that! I'm such an idiot," or some variation therein, you're holding a grudge against yourself. If you've ever said, "What a b****! I'm never going to forgive her," then you're holding a grudge against another. For this reason, I recommend that you forgive all - both others and yourself. Let bygones be bygones, as they say. Nothing lets your heart relax and unload its long-standing stress better than just letting go of any animosity against anyone.

Let it all go - BOOM! Just like that, you can choose to forgive the person who abused you, the kid who bullied you, the girl who broke your heart. Who cares who was right or wrong? Just let it go. We're all human and we all make mistakes; that's how we learn. No matter if it was 30 years ago or last week, *let it go*. Just as in meditation, you're going to let it slide so you can focus your mind on the present and immediate future. Please note that this isn't the same as forgetting; you do not ever have to forget that someone has wronged you, or is an energy vampire. Odds are, you need to limit your interactions with people who have harmed you previously, unless they prove that they are on a similar path to loving themselves, too.

Dr. Kousouli's Secret Loving Self Tip #28
ALWAYS TALK TO YOURSELF POSITIVELY

There is one thing I know for sure: You deserve so much love! I ask that you honor yourself and treat yourself like you would treat a best friend. Why not constantly talk to yourself in a loving way? So you messed up? No worries! You will do better next time. Forgot where you put your keys? No, you are not stupid, you're human, so you're allowed to make mistakes and learn from them - the keys will show up at some point. Listen *very* carefully to the way you talk about yourself in these minor instances, because they are a signal for how you talk to yourself when things really hit the fan.

Here is a simple exercise for picking yourself up any time you are feeling down. Do this at a time when you're really happy and positive about yourself and life. Record your own voice into your cell phone recorder application. Talk nicely to yourself on your cell phone recorder for about two to five minutes saying beautiful things like, "I am a positive loving person and deserve all the good God has for me." Whenever you are feeling down, you can simply pull out the positive file and play it back to yourself. Give yourself a nice pep talk before the big game, test, or any life challenge from the most important person in your world - YOU!

Train the voice in your head to be positive, and release all self-rejection and negative programming. Read *BE A MASTER*™ *OF PSYCHIC ENERGY* for help in releasing yourself from dogmatic religious, parental, or other old social pre-programming and learn to control the negative ego.

Dr. Kousouli's Secret Loving Self Tip #29
PLANT POSITIVE SAYINGS ALL OVER YOUR HOUSE

One of the best ways to change your inner monologue is to change the constant input you give yourself. Compliment yourself by writing sticky notes and putting them all over your place. On the mirror, on your desk, on the fridge, in the bathroom, everywhere. Write nice things like "Hey cutie," or "You look beautiful today." If you have an important job interview coming up, write "You can do it!" There are plenty of great DIY art projects you can do, too, from painting inspirational quotes on canvas to making your own In-vision board.

Your brain is constantly taking cues from the environment around you, even when you're not consciously aware of it. You will absorb positive messages even when you're doing something else, and you will continue to grow even when you're not trying.

A great book chalk full of activities to love yourself and others daily, is "LOVE, You. Me. We." by Arielle Caputo.

Dr. Kousouli's Secret Loving Self Tip #30
BE GRATEFUL AND APPRECIATIVE

Some people didn't get the honor of waking up today. You did. This means you're lucky enough to create for yet another day here in paradise. We don't have the luxury of damning any circumstances in our lives; doing so is essentially denying our gift of life. Instead of being ungrateful, we must see everything as a blessing to experience, and be grateful for the chance to grow from every opportunity we face. So be grateful, and hopefully tomorrow you'll get another day. You never know when your time to create on this earth is over, so don't take a chance to create positivity and make a difference for granted.

Use this in your meditation and journal/notebook as well. Even writing down three things you're grateful for in the morning and in the evening can increase feelings of gratitude and improve your mood. Even on your worst day, you have at least three things to be grateful for, including the fact that you're still alive. Live in gratitude, and receive abundance. For some of us, this is more difficult than we would expect, though.

> ## Dr. Kousouli's Secret Loving Self Tip #31
> ## NEGOTIATE HARD WITH THE EGO

If your ego is out of control, you must learn this little trick called "ego negotiation." This is when we treat our egos as little kids and give them what they want, but ONLY when we, the parent (the higher mind), get what we want first. "You can have the cookie, but only after we do our chores and workout regimen for the day." The cookie is a reward for good work. If you let the ego get its way without the higher mind negotiating for the betterment of you first, you will slip into the ego's master plan of always sabotaging your success and forward movement. Everything is negotiable. Let the ego wait, and cater to the higher mind's wishes first, you'll always be glad you did in the long run.

Chapter Eleven:
Choose the Energy You Let into Your Space

"Distracted from distraction by distraction."
~ *T.S. Eliot*

A side from the work you must perform on yourself, and the efforts you must place into weeding out the energy vampires in your life, you must also address other external forces. Our minds are entirely susceptible to messages from the outside world, just as I mentioned in the previous chapter when it comes to surrounding yourself with positive messages. Unfortunately, the majority of what we see and absorb is *not* positive, and comes in the form of thought control from the massive amounts of media we consume. I go into this topic in depth in my books *BE A MASTER™ OF SUCCESS and BE A MASTER™ OF PSYCHIC ENERGY*, if you'd like to work towards removing thought control from your life all together.

Dr. Kousouli's Secret Loving Self Tip #32
EASE UP ON ALL SOCIAL MEDIA

Gasp! "But Dr. Kousouli! That is impossible!" People tend to get a little touchy about giving up their social media, but you'd be amazed at what a "social media detox" can do for your mind. Okay, okay, you don't have to give it up forever, but if you do this from time to time, you'll learn you *can* actually live without habitually checking for new updates, tweets, or likes. Hire a media company to help you manage your social media and get out there and talk to REAL people! Go for a walk *outside* without burying your face in your phone.

Most of the depressive states people find themselves in are due to a disconnection in real life. Maybe you feel like a loner, or like you're not worthy of love, or like no one else understands you. That's the beauty of the Internet; you can find people that seem just like you, who understand, and who can talk to you daily without ever really needing to meet face-to-face. This is a farce, though, because only real human connection can be made when you allow yourself to be vulnerable enough to meet someone in person.

On top of that, when you're on social media nonstop, you're only seeing the lives that people *want* you to see; not the ones they actually live. It's crazy how much of what we see isn't actually real, but we think it is, and compare ourselves to an unrealistic goal of "who we should be." Guess what!? Someone out there will "like" the real you if you give them the chance. Getting to know people in person is much better than getting a like on your profile picture, and building a connection with someone in person is much more gratifying than another friend request from a stranger.

Dr. Kousouli's Secret Loving Self Tip #33
DROP ALL NEGATIVE TV, MOVIES, AND INTERNET

Have you ever noticed how media in general makes you feel after you interact with it? Do you feel anxious or worried after watching a news broadcast about "mounting tensions in the Middle East"? Do you feel angry when you browse your social media feeds during election season and all of your "friends" are sharing their opinions? Do you watch movies that are highly sexual or violent in nature that desensitize you to negative energy and behaviors? If you answered yes to any of these questions, you're not alone. I have found many patients with current day anxiety and fears are connected to a long-standing history of media hypnosis as children, when they were traumatized by media and are now attracted to drama and pain in their lives without realizing it. They have allowed for creation of an old subconscious, continuous, paralyzing loop of fear and chaos that, unknown to them, is adding unnecessary stress to their already toxic lives.

Our media is so powerful, and is responsible for much of our behavior in life. Humans are easily hypnotized; all you have to do is attract our attention and we're immediately swayed. There are methods of thought control that are used in our daily media, from the bright flickering lights and loud startling sounds on the TV, to the way our favorite websites are designed to sway our eyes. Take a moment to step back and decide, just like you did with your friends and family, which of these media sources is an energy vampire, and which is a positive source of energy. Don't let your mind be programmed by mass media, as its agenda is to sway you from your personal mission and happiness.

Chapter Twelve:
Conclusion

"Discarding the person you were made to be, will bring some very interesting conversation between you and your maker one day."
~ Dr. Theo Kousouli

How can we improve the course of humanity for future generations? How do we spread the message of love instead of hate and abuse? Show compassion; it starts with you being the example. Don't perpetuate the mind virus of abuse, even if you have been badly abused by another. We must all choose to allow the blessings of forgiveness and compassion into our lives. If connected to forgiveness and compassion for yourself and others, you will see the world anew from a higher "victim-free" perspective. You will fall in love with you, everyone, and everything. To do this, there must be an uninterrupted connection of unity and understanding with the higher power inside you - no matter what the activity you are doing. The spark of greatness lives inside you. You are never alone, and The Creator is in everything we do; in every minute, every second, twenty four hours a day, three hundred sixty five days a year; while driving, working, sleeping, and reading, etc. - in everything, always.

All the masters of spiritual awareness showed immense levels of forgiveness and compassion. When you love with compassion you are part of the whole, and you are not separated or misplaced in the universe. Those who hold compassion and forgiveness in their heart change not only their own future but the future of our world.

I hope that this book has empowered you towards truly embracing life to the fullest. We have all had terrible things happen in our lives, and some of us were exposed to trauma that others can't even imagine. But no matter who you are, where you come from, or what your story is, I do know this: You shall overcome. In order to do so, you must be able to look yourself in the mirror every day and love the person staring back at you. We are all worthy of love.

Way, way easier said than done, right? But the tools in this book will help you do just that. Even if you find yourself thinking, "That's too much work," or, "That's too cheesy/hippie/weird," just *try* what has been discussed in these pages. You never know what's going to work for you unless you give it a wholehearted attempt. I know that working on your body through chiropractic care, exercise, and a healthy diet will work wonders for you, but it's not the whole game. You also need to approach your struggles from a mental and spiritual approach as well, or you won't be able to fix the whole issue. You are the sum of all your healthy parts, not just the broken pieces.

What I wish for you most is that you love yourself thoroughly, as the Creator surely does!

See you at the seminars!

In the highest vibration of love and light for you - God bless,

Theodoros Kousouli D.C., CHt.

About the Author

A holistic health care advisor, teacher, speaker, mentor and author who is featured on major networks, Theodoros Kousouli D.C., CHt., is Los Angeles' premier holistic metaphysical energy healer. He is recognized and trusted for effective, quick, drug-free results. His remarkable natural, pain-free, holistic healing system - the Kousouli® Method - focuses on getting patients to their top performance levels by unblocking pathways using the body's own repair mechanisms.

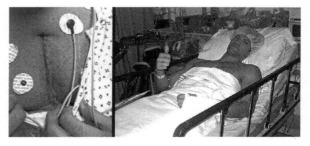

His desire to help others stems from his personal journey recovering from semi-paralysis and major heart surgery, and includes everything he's learned about the optimum wellness techniques that define his practice.

Dr. Theo Kousouli is the author of *five previous books,* including: *BE A MASTER™ of PSYCHIC ENERGY and BE A MASTER™ of MAXIMUM HEALING.* A personal coach and advisor to entertainers, business leaders, energy healers, and spiritual seekers of all varieties, Dr. Kousouli holds seminars teaching people how to tap into their inner healing and higher-level abilities through the use of their nervous systems. Visit **www.KousouliMethod.com** for more information on developing your intuition and personal power to live a more purpose-filled, meaningful, and healthy life. Dr. Kousouli is the ideal speaker for your next event.

To Schedule Dr. Theo Kousouli For Your Next Event:

www.DrKousouli.com

Life Changing Products · Books · Seminars · Empowerment CD's · Get on the Newsletter!
Connect with Dr. Kousouli, www.DrKousouli.com and on all Social Media Platforms
@DrKousouli #DrKousouli #KousouliMethod
You Will Also Enjoy Dr. Kousouli's Other Published Works
Available Now from Major Retailers:

BE A MASTER™ OF MAXIMUM HEALING
How to Lead a Healthy Life Without Limits

- Holistic Solutions for Over <u>60</u> Diseases to Help You and Your Loved Ones Heal!

BE A MASTER™ OF PSYCHIC ENERGY
Your Key to Truly Mastering Your Personal Power

- Uncover and Amplify Your Hidden Psychic Abilities to Change Your Life!

BE A MASTER™ OF SEX ENERGY
Hypnotize Your Partner for Love and Great Sex

- Build a Stronger Bond with Your Lover(s) Using Subconscious Science!

BE A MASTER™ OF SUCCESS
Dr.Kousouli's 33 Master Secrets to Achieving Your Dreams

- Solid Success Principles You can Apply Right Now to Empower Your Life!

BE A MASTER™ OF SELF IMAGE
Dr.Kousouli's 33 Master Secrets to Living Healthier, Happier and Hotter

- Simple Holistic Tips & Tricks for More Weight Loss and Body Benefit to You!

If you would like to share your story of how Dr. Kousouli's books, CDs or seminars have impacted your life for the better, we would love to hear from you! (Messages are screened by staff and forwarded when appropriate.)

For A Free Gift from Dr. Theo Kousouli visit www.FreeGiftFromDrTheo.com

69549153R00055

Made in the USA
San Bernardino, CA
17 February 2018